# HITLER'S
## STOLEN CHILDREN

The Shocking True Story of the
Nazi Kidnapping Conspiracy

INGRID VON OELHAFEN & TIM TATE

*with*

Dr. Dorothee Schmitz-Köster

## Collins

Published by Collins, an imprint of HarperCollins Publishers Ltd

Originally published in the UK by Elliott & Thompson in 2015
under the title *Hitler's Forgotten Children*
First published in Canada by Collins in this trade paperback edition: 2020

HarperCollins books may be purchased for educational, business,
or sales promotional use through our Special Markets Department.

HarperCollins Publishers Ltd
Bay Adelaide Centre, East Tower
22 Adelaide Street West, 41st Floor
Toronto, Ontario, Canada
M5H 4E3

*www.harpercollins.ca*

Library and Archives Canada Cataloguing in Publication information
is available upon request.

Book design by Tiffany Estreicher

ISBN 978-1-4434-6063-7

Printed and bound in the United States of America

LSC/C  10  9  8  7  6  5  4  3  2  1

*This book is dedicated to all the victims of Nazi Germany—men, women, and above all, children—and to those throughout the world today who suffer from the persisting evil that teaches that one race, creed, or color is superior to another.*

# PREFACE

B LOOD.
    Blood runs through this story. The blood of young men spilled on the battlefields of war; the blood of civilians—old and young, women and men—that ran in the gutters of cities, towns, and villages across Europe; the blood of millions destroyed in the pogroms and death camps of the Holocaust.

But blood, too, as an idea. The Nazi belief—absurd and obscene as this seems today—in "good blood," precious ichor to be sought out, preserved, and expanded. And with it, the inevitable counterpart: "bad blood," to be identified and then ruthlessly eradicated.

I am a child—a German child—of a war based on and steeped in blood. I was born in 1941 in the depths of the Second World War: I grew up in its wake—and under the shadow of its brutal and even more prolonged progeny, the Cold War.

My history is the history of millions of men and women like me. We are the victims of Hitler's obsession with blood, as well as the beneficiaries of the postwar economic miracle that transformed our devastated and pariah nation into the powerhouse of modern Europe.

Our story is that of a generation raised in the shadow of bloody infamy, but one that found a way to struggle toward honesty and decency.

But my own story is also that of a much more secret past: a history still cloaked in silence and shrouded in shame. It is a warning of what happens when blood is worshiped as the vital essence that determines human worth, and—by extension—used as the justification for the most terrible crimes man has inflicted upon man.

For I am a child of Lebensborn.

*Lebensborn* is an ancient German word, twisted and distorted by the word-smelters of National Socialism into a uniquely disturbing shape amid the vast and bizarre vocabulary of Hitler's Reich. What did it mean in the mad lexicon of Nazism? What does it mean today? To find the answers—to uncover my own story—has taken me on a long and painful journey: a physical journey, to be sure, which has led me across the map of modern Europe. An historical expedition, too: one that has required an often uncomfortable return to the Germany of more than seventy years ago, and into the troubled stories of those countries overrun by Hitler's armies.

But the search for who I am, and who I have been, has also forced me to make a psychological voyage into everything I have known and grown up with: a fundamental questioning of who I am, and what it means to be German.

I will not pretend that this is an easy story: it will not—cannot— always be easy to read. But as—if—you do, please keep in mind that neither has it been an easy story to live.

I am not, by nature, overtly emotional. The expression of emotion— such a commonplace in twenty-first-century society—does not come effortlessly to me. I have, I think, spent my life attempting to suppress my inner self, to subordinate my feelings to the circumstances in which I have grown up, as well as to the needs of others.

But this is a story that, I believe strongly, needs to be heard. More, much more, it needs to be understood. It is not unique, if by that we mean that there are others who have endured much of what has shaped my life and times. But, perhaps in defiance of the strict definition, there are, in life, gradations of uniqueness: and so, while I share a common thread with thousands of others who passed through the vile and perverse experiment of Lebensborn, to the best of my knowledge no one else shares the particular twists of fate, history, and geography that have defined my seventy-four years on earth.

*LEBENSBORN.* THE WORD runs through my life like the blood coursing through my body; a mysterious and powerful river, its route and progress obscure to the naked eye. To see it, to understand it, demands much more than a superficial examination: to find its source—and thus the roots of this story—requires a deep and intrusive investigation into the most hidden places.

And we must start in a town and a country that no longer exist.

# ONE

## August 1942

*Men . . . must be shot, the women locked up and transported to concentration camps, and the children must be torn from their motherland and instead accommodated in the territories of the old Reich.*

REICHSFÜHRER SS HEINRICH HIMMLER,
*June 25, 1942*

CILLI, GERMAN-OCCUPIED YUGOSLAVIA:

*August 3–7, 1942*

THE SCHOOL YARD was crowded. Hundreds of women—young and old—clutched the hands of their children and found what space they could in the packed courtyard; nearby, Wehrmacht soldiers, rifles slung over their shoulders, looked on as the families slowly drifted in from towns and villages across the area.

These women had been summoned by order of their new German masters, ordered to bring their children to the school for "medical tests." Upon arrival they were arrested and told to wait. Otto Lurker, commander of the police and security services for the region, watched, relaxed and impassive—his hands resting comfortably in his pockets—as the yard filled with families. Once, Lurker had been Hitler's jailer; now he was the Führer's leading henchman in Lower Styria. He held the rank of SS *Standartenführer*—the paramilitary equivalent of a full colonel in the army—but that summer's morning he was casually dressed in a two-piece civilian suit.

Yugoslavia had been under Nazi rule for sixteen months. In March 1941, as the surrounding countries of Hungary, Romania, and

Bulgaria joined the Reich's alliance of Balkan nations, Hitler put pressure on the kingdom's ruler, the Regent Prince Paul, to fall into line. The prince and his cabinet bowed to the inevitable, formally tying Yugoslavia to the Axis Powers: but the Serb-dominated army launched a coup d'état, replacing Paul with his seventeen-year-old second cousin, Prince Peter.

News of the revolt reached Berlin on March 27. Hitler took the coup as a personal insult and issued Directive 25, formally designating the country as an enemy of the Reich. The Führer ordered his armies "to destroy Yugoslavia militarily and as a state." A week later, the Luftwaffe began a devastating bombing campaign while divisions of Wehrmacht infantry and tanks of the Panzer Corps swept through towns and villages. The Royal Yugoslavian Army was no match for German's Blitzkrieg troops: on April 17, the country surrendered.

The occupying troops immediately set about fulfilling Hitler's instruction to dismantle all vestiges of the state. Sixty-five thousand people—primarily intellectuals and nationalists—were exiled, imprisoned, or murdered, their homes and property handed over to the new German masters. The Slovene language was prohibited.

But for the rest of 1941 and throughout the first half of 1942, partisan groups, led by the Communist Josip Broz Tito, fought a determined campaign of resistance. Germany retaliated with a brutal crackdown: the Gestapo swooped on fighters and civilians alike, deporting thousands to concentration camps across the Reich. Others were selected to be executed as a warning against resistance. In a nine-month period beginning in September 1941, 374 men and women were lined up against the walls of the prison yard at Cilli and summarily shot. Photographers recorded the murders for posterity and propaganda.

On June 25, 1942, Heinrich Himmler—the second most powerful

and feared man in Nazi Germany—issued orders to his secret police and SS officers to eliminate partisan resistance.

*This campaign possesses every required element to make harmless the population which has supported the bandits and provided them with human resources, weapons and shelter. Men from such families, and often even their relatives, must be shot, the women locked up and transported to concentration camps, and the children must be torn from their motherland and instead accommodated in the territories of the old Reich. I expect to be provided with a special report on the number of children and their racial values.*

Against this bloody backdrop, 1,262 people—many the surviving relatives of the partisans executed as an example to the rest of the population—assembled in the school yard that August morning to await their fate.

Among them was a family from the nearby village of Sauerbrunn. Johann Matko came from a family of known partisans: his brother, Ignaz, had been one of those lined up and shot against the wall of Cilli Prison in July and he had been dragged off to Mauthausen concentration camp. After seven months he was allowed to return home to his wife, Helena, and their three children: eight-year-old Tanja, her brother Ludwig—then six—and nine-month-old baby Erika.

When all the families were accounted for, an order was given to separate them into three groups—one each for the children, the women, and the men. Under Lurker's direction the soldiers moved in and pulled children from the grasp of their mothers: a local photographer, Josip Pelikan, recorded the harrowing scene for the Reich's obsessive archivists. His rolls of film captured the fear and alarm of women and children alike; Pelikan also snapped off shots of scores toddlers held in low pens of straw inside the school buildings.

As the mothers waited outside, Nazi officials began a cursory examination of the children. Working with charts and clipboards, they painstakingly noted down each child's facial and physical characteristics.

These, though, were not "medical tests" as any doctor would know them; instead they were crude assessments of "racial value" that assigned each youngster to one of four categories. Those who met Himmler's strict criteria for what a child of true German blood should look like were placed in Category 1 or 2: this formally registered them as potentially useful additions to the Reich population. By contrast, any hint or trace of Slavic features—and certainly any sign of "Jewish heritage"— caused a child to be consigned to the lowest racial status of Categories 3 and 4. Thus branded as *Untermensch*, they had no value except as future slave labor for the Nazi state.

By the following day this rudimentary sifting was finished. Some children—those deemed racially worthless—were handed back to their families. But 430 other youngsters—from young babies to twelve-year-old boys and girls—were taken away by their captors. Rounded up by nurses from the German Red Cross, they were packed into trains and transported across the Yugoslavian border to an *Umsiedlunslager*—or transit camp—at Frohnleiten, near the Austrian town of Graz.

They did not stay long in this holding center. By September 1942 a further selection had been made—this time by trained "race assessors" from one of the myriad organizations established by Himmler to preserve and strengthen the pool of "good blood."

Noses were measured and compared to the official ideal length and shape; lips, teeth, hips, and genitals were likewise prodded, poked, and photographed to sort the genetically precious human wheat from the less valuable chaff. This finer, more rigorous sieving was used to reassign the captives to the four racial categories.

Older children newly listed in Categories 3 or 4 were shipped off to reeducation camps across Bavaria in the very heartland of Nazi Germany. The best of the younger ones in the top two categories would—in time—be handed over to a secretive project run by the *Reichsführer* himself. Its name was *Lebensborn*; and among the infants assigned to its care was a nine-month-old baby called Erika Matko.

TWO

---

# 1945—Year Zero

---

*It is our will that this state shall endure for a thousand years.*

*We are happy to know that the future is ours entirely!*

ADOLF HITLER,

*TRIUMPH OF THE WILL, 1935*

A T 2:40 A.M. on Monday, May 7, 1945, in a small, redbrick schoolhouse in the French city of Reims, Generaloberst Alfred Jodl, chief of operations for the German Armed Forces High Command, signed the unconditional surrender of the Thousand Year Reich. The five terse paragraphs of this act of capitulation handed over Germany and all its inhabitants to the mercy of the four victorious Allied Powers—Britain, America, France, and the Soviet Union—from 11:01 p.m. the following night.

A week earlier, Hitler and most of his inner circle had committed suicide in the bowels of the Berlin *Führerbunker*. His chief henchman, SS Reichsführer Heinrich Himmler—the man in charge of the entire Nazi apparatus of terror—was on the run, disguised in the coarse gray serge of an enlisted soldier and equipped with forged papers proclaiming him to be a humble sergeant.

It was over; six years of "total war" in which my country had murdered and plundered its way across Europe were finished. Now we had to live with the peace.

Who were we that May morning? What was Germany—once the begetter of Bach and Beethoven, Goethe and Schiller—in the aftermath of the brutality of the Blitzkrieg, let alone the filth and genocide of the Final Solution? What would peace look like to the victors and to the vanquished? Those would prove to be two very different questions, linked by a common answer.

A new term was coined to describe our situation in 1945: *die Stunde Null*. Literally translated, this means "zero hour"; but for the smoldering remains of Germany—a country of ruins, shame, and starvation—it was more accurately "year zero": both an end and a beginning.

What did it mean to be a German from 11:01 p.m. on Tuesday, May 8, 1945? To the Allies—the new owners of every meter of turf and of every individual life from the Mass in the west to the Memel in the east—it meant subjugation, suspicion, and suppression. Never again, said the four occupying powers, would the poisonous twin rivers of German nationalism and militarism be allowed to rise up and flood across the continent. There would, within hours, be mechanisms and procedures put in place to enforce this noble ideal—systems that, though I was too young to know then, would direct the course of my life.

To GERMANS, THIS existential question of identity meant something different again. Something much less philosophical, something that could be categorized as the three P's: physical, political, and psychological. And of this trinity, the greatest—the most pressing—was undoubtedly the physical.

Germany in May 1945 was a wasteland; a tortured tundra of

blown-up bridges, torn-up roads, burned-out tanks. In the dying weeks and months of his Reich, consumed by madness and impotent rage, Hitler had issued orders to create "fortress cities." The Fatherland, he pronounced, was to be defended to the last drop of pure German blood and the last brick of German building. There was to be no surrender, but, instead, a *Götterdämmerung* of flame and sacrifice to mark the final days of his self-proclaimed Master Race.

The result was less a noble funeral pyre than a thousand-mile-wide bonfire of his vanity. Forced to fight for every inch of territory— and bludgeoned by Allied carpet-bombing—Germany was reduced to a post-apocalyptic desert. The once-mighty Reich buildings were reduced to piles of rubble; in Berlin alone there were seventy-five million tons of it piled up along and across almost every street. And as Berlin, so, too, the rest of the German cities; destroyed and obliterated by bombing and house-to-house fighting that damaged or left derelict 70 percent of all their buildings. And everywhere, now hollow-eyed and haggard, the once-arrogant people who had subjugated those they believed to be inferior races to the iron destiny of Germany's future.

Newsreels and photos—Allied ones, since the German press had been shut down from the moment of surrender—captured previously unimaginable scenes. Clustered around half-destroyed buildings, blown apart so that glimpses of a once normal life—a fireplace, shreds of wallpaper, the remains of a toilet—gaped obscenely in the absence of their protective walls, were the living ghosts of women and children. Orphans, refugees, the aged and the wounded; everywhere a dystopian tableau of anonymous bodies lying in the street, watched— or more often avoided—by skeletal figures who might well soon join them in death.

What were they—what were we—doing? All of Germany, at least in the cities, was picking through debris, creating makeshift shelters, scrounging for food and either hiding from or fearfully fraternizing with the victorious occupying armies. Not from choice but from necessity. For there was one thing missing more vital even than shelter: food.

In the last weeks of the war, the country's economy—so long directed by and for the benefit of the Nazi party—had collapsed as completely as its buildings. Ironically, there was plenty of money, but the wads of paper and mounds of coin were useless; as every available resource was diverted away from the people to the needs of the army, and as explosions ripped up the railway network, preventing what food was harvested from being distributed, there was little or nothing to buy with the now-useless marks.

Nor did our new masters appear to have a coherent idea of what to do with us. Between July and August 1945, the Allied leaders—Churchill, Truman, and Stalin—met at Potsdam to plan the future. Unlike the end of the First World War, when Germany was defeated and subjected to severe punishment and reparations but not wiped from the geographical and political map, at Potsdam the decision was taken that the country would cease to exist once the war against Hitler ended. In its place there would be four separate "occupation zones," each owned and ruled by one of the war's victors, according to its own unique principles and plans.

But beyond that there had been little concerted thinking about what, practically, would be done with the former German state once Hitler and his thugs had been defeated. France had favored breaking the Reich into a series of small independent states, while the United States had considered returning Germany to the condition of a preindustrialized nation focused and dependent on farming. Washington would come to relent, to accept that requiring tens of millions of

Germans to live as medieval peasants was unworkable as well as undesirable. But the Allies failed to contemplate how their separate occupations would function, and none of their plans addressed the monumental problem of feeding both a conquered people—a population swelled by more than ten million refugees from the east—and the massive armies imposing the peace.

Food: there was simply not enough of it—and without a functioning transport system, what little there was couldn't be moved to the places where it was most needed. Worse, there was a widespread feeling among the occupying armies that Germans were long overdue a taste of their own medicine; had the Nazi rampage across Europe not deliberately starved villages, towns, cities, and entire nations to the point of death? Wasn't it time for Germany to reap what she had sown?

This, then, was Hitler's true legacy: a nation starving—and being starved—to death; a population reduced to a desperate struggle for survival in which men, women, and children subsisted on half the calories needed to sustain life. At best. A country not simply beaten and half destroyed but wiped completely out of existence.

I was three and a half when peace came. A small, quiet, and archetypally blond German child, living in Bandekow, a tiny hamlet in the rural heart of the Mecklenburg region, with my mother, grandmother, and slightly older brother Dietmar. Our home was a big farmhouse, half timbered and characteristic of the region, set in acres of forest. We were, I think, typical both of a particular class of prewar Germans and, by contrast, of the postwar country at large. On both sides—maternal and paternal—our family was old, well established, and, notwithstanding the wrecked economy, well off.

My mother, Gisela, was the daughter of a shipping line magnate from Hamburg. The Andersens belonged to the old Hanseatic class—the patrician and prestigious ruling elite that had made its money and its name from trade since the Congress of Vienna declared Hamburg a free city in 1815.

Our house in Bandekow had been in my mother's family for generations; it belonged to my grandmother's brother, but had almost certainly been used as a country retreat in the years before 1945. Certainly the Andersens kept their main residence in Hamburg itself, and my grandfather remained there, with my grandmother dividing her time between the two homes.

Gisela was one of four Andersen children. Her brother had been killed, serving in the Wehrmacht in the last days of the war; her eldest sister was estranged—the result of some unspoken act of dishonesty that tarnished the otherwise respectable family name—but her remaining sibling, my aunt Ingrid (known universally as Erika, or "Eka"), was a constant companion in my childhood.

At the end of the war, Gisela was thirty-one: young, bright—albeit in the brittle and privileged way of her class—and pretty. She was also married—and not, as it turned out, happily.


HERMANN VON OELHAFEN was a career soldier. He had served with honor in the First War; he was seriously injured in 1914, again in 1915, and, after a final wound in 1917, was awarded the Iron Cross for his pains. Like Gisela, he came from an aristocratic background: both his father and his mother could boast the telltale *von*—a signifier of the upper class—in their family names.

But where Gisela was young and lively, Hermann was the complete opposite. He was thirty years older than Gisela and suffered from severe epileptic seizures. Whether these were the cause of his peevish, mean-spirited nature I do not know; what I am certain of is that their marriage—which took place in 1935, during the first confident years of Hitler's reign—was, by 1945, effectively over. As I grew from being a toddler to a young child, I rarely saw my father; while we lived in the farmhouse at Bandekow, Hermann lived a thousand kilometers away in the Bavarian town of Ansbach.

Perhaps outwardly there was nothing strange in Gisela—a married woman—living alone with her children and mother. In this our little family was all too typical of our now-dissolved nation in the immediate months after the war: most adult men—even the very young and the elderly—had been drafted into military service and were now either dead, missing, or locked up in prisoner-of-war camps across Europe. Germany was a country—more accurately, a former country—of women and children.

But though, as we shall see, it played its part, the war was not the prime reason for the separation of my parents. There was simply an unbridgeable gulf between them—an emotional fracture even less open to resolution than the divisions imposed upon their nation. I was then too young to know this, but it would, in time, come to render my childhood as bleak as the politically deteriorating situation in which we found ourselves. Bleaker, probably.

Politics. The second P that defined life at the end of the war. Not politics as modern generations have come to know and disregard it; not the jockeying for position and power between rival parties in a settled democracy—no, politics in 1945 was red in tooth and claw.

The last days of the war had seen the Allied forces smashing their way through Germany from all parts of the compass. American tanks and troops rolled eastward from France, Belgium, and Holland; the British fought their way northward, up through the country from Italy and Austria; and the vast armies of the Soviet Union raced westward from what had been, before the war, Poland. For each there was an overriding imperative to conquer and control as much German territory as possible; whatever they held when the war finally ended would, under the Potsdam agreement become their property with very little prospect of any subsequent redistribution. In those last weeks of spring 1945 the borders of postwar Europe were being re-created—and, at the same time, the seeds of what would shortly be known as the Cold War were being planted.

When the fighting was over, it turned out that my father's home was in the American zone; henceforth his fate would depend on the way Washington viewed its duties and rights over the territory it now owned. But Bandekow, where I lived with my mother, grandmother, and Dietmar, my slightly elder brother, was in the Soviet occupation zone, and Moscow had very different ideas about how to dismantle the infrastructure of Nazi Germany—as well as what it wanted to do with its share of the former Reich.

Initially, at least, there was agreement between the Allies on the need to bring Hitler's surviving henchmen to justice. A four-power war crimes tribunal was established to put the National Socialist machine on trial; Göring, Jodl, Hess, von Ribbentrop, and twenty other leaders of the National Socialist state were locked up in cells beneath the Palace of Justice in Nuremberg to await trial for crimes of war and crimes against humanity. Other than Hitler and Goebbels, the most notable absentee from this roll call of infamy was Himmler: the man who had created the SS and who had masterminded the entire apparatus of Nazi terror, had committed suicide before he could be transported to Nuremberg.

The eventual trial and conviction of these vicious war criminals was undoubtedly a triumph for justice, but it also marked the high point of cooperation between the occupying powers. After Nuremberg, America, Britain, France, and the Soviet Union would each take a radically different approach to ruling the land and populations they controlled; the individual fates of tens of millions of former Germans depended on which zone they happened to have been in when the war ended. Very soon these great political divides would change forever the lives of our little family.

The contrast between the four occupying powers was played out first in the way they viewed those who had been members of the Nazi Party. *Denazification* was a term coined in Washington during the last years of war: President Franklin Roosevelt and his successor, Harry Truman, recognized that the party's tendrils had wound themselves throughout every aspect of German life, from the political to the judicial, from the public to the personal. In May 1945 there were more than eight million members of the Nazi Party—around 10 percent of the total population. What was to be done about this entwining of the mechanics of fascism with the warp and weft of everyday life?

The search for an answer was not, of course, confined to America. Each of the Allied powers now controlled its own swath of Germany; each faced the problem of how to pull out the roots of National Socialism and yet somehow ensure that their own zone of occupation kept functioning.

The first step was to outlaw the party. On September 20, 1945, Control Council Proclamation No. 2 announced that *"The National*

*Socialist German Workers Party (NSDAP) is completely and finally abolished and declared to be illegal"* throughout all the former Reich.

But the party itself was only the most visible of a byzantine tangle of Nazi organizations. Beneath it were more than sixty other official associations, ranging from internationally notorious bodies like the SS, Gestapo, and Hitler Youth to much more obscure societies (even within Germany) such as the Reich Committee for the Protection of German Blood and the Deutsche Frauenschaft, the National Socialist Women's Movement. All were duly made illegal; more importantly, previous association with any one of them would be enough to flag a member as someone to be suspected as a Nazi sympathizer.

Neither Hermann nor Gisela was—to the best of my knowledge— a party member. Neither did I ever hear them express fascist opinions or support for Hitler. But their personal histories—my father as a career soldier, who had been a desk officer in the Wehrmacht for much of the war, my mother as a former member of Deutsche Frauenschaft—must have led to some investigations by denazification officials of their respective occupation zones.

AND THIS IS where the divergence in approach between the American rulers of my father's region and the Soviet masters who now controlled the area in which my mother, Dietmar, and I lived, would determine the differing courses of our lives.

The Americans were initially fiercely committed to denazification, but then became the most pragmatic of the occupying armies. Washington's military government realized quickly that, however desirable, widespread purges of suspected Nazis would mean that the entire responsibility for organizing day-to-day life fell exclusively on its shoulders—a burden that, for a war-weary nation anxious to bring its troops home, was simply too onerous.

And so while my father, like every adult living in the American zone, was required to fill out a questionnaire (termed variously a *Fragebogen* or a *Meldebogen*) in which he affirmed that he was not, and never had been, a member of any Nazi organization, there was little follow-up or detailed examination of these self-declarations. With little or no oversight, most applicants were issued official documents pronouncing them to be "good Germans," free of the stain of fascism. They quickly became known as *Persilschein*—pieces of paper that were able to wash the past as clean as any soap powder.

BUT THE SOVIET approach was very much less relaxed. Perhaps because it had suffered greater losses and devastation than any of the four Allied Powers—or more likely, because Stalin had a very clear idea of the future for the Soviet zone—Moscow adopted a very much less permissive approach.

The Soviet military administration in Germany—known by its acronym, SMAD—controlled a vast swath of territory from the Oder River in the east to the Elbe in the west. On April 18, 1945, Lavrenti Beria—Stalin's much-feared head of the secret police—issued order Number 00315; it mandated the immediate internment of active Nazis and senior members of party organizations; no investigations were required prior to these arrests. From the start of May, the first of an eventual 123,000 Germans were rounded up and incarcerated in ten special camps set up across the Soviet zone.

The existence of these prisons—run by the NKVD, Stalin's equivalent of the Gestapo and frequently on the site of former Nazi concentration camps—was in itself a secret. No contact was to be allowed between those held there and the outside world, but inevitably word did leak out; the often random nature of arrests and internment—by February 1946, genuine party members formed less than half of the total number of prisoners—fear of being dragged off to the network of *Schweigelager* (literally: "Silence Camps") weighed heavily on the already fearful German population under Soviet military rule.

Almost anything—anonymous denunciation, previous membership in an obscure Nazi society, or contact with anyone in the other three occupation zones—was enough to earn a knock on the door and transport to a *Schweigelager*. All too often this proved to be a one-way ticket: almost forty-three thousand men and women would die behind the barbed wire of these postwar concentration camps.

Did my mother worry incessantly about the risk her involvement with Deutsche Frauenschaft posed to her and our little household in Bandekow? I do not know: the von Oelhafens were a closemouthed family, never given to open discussions of emotions, much less of the past. But I know something now that I did not know—could not have known—then: a secret at the heart of my childhood that tied Gisela, Hermann, and me to one of the most sinister of all Nazi organizations, and one that would certainly have spelled trouble for us if SMAD came to hear of it.

Was this an added worry, clouding my mother's mind? Again, I do not know. What I do know is that as summer turned to winter that eventful year of 1945, Gisela was terrified. And her fear had a name: rape.

Throughout 1945, as the Soviet Army fought its way into Germany, its troops mastered one phrase above all: *Komm, Frau*. It was an order that brooked no disobedience and one that led to the same inevitable conclusion.

Tens of thousands—perhaps ten times that number—of German women paid, with their bodies, the price for Hitler's appalling brutal treatment of Russian cities and populations. Rape was so commonplace in the Soviet sector—so much so that it ceased to be news—that for women and girls anywhere between puberty and old age the question was not *whether* they had been violated but *how many* times.

It was also quasi-officially sanctioned. Although SMAD commanders in some parts of the occupied zone paid lip service to stamping out the violation of German women, in reality others paid a heavy price for doing so. One young Red Army captain, Lev Kopelev, intervened to stop the gang rape of a group of girls and was sentenced for his troubles to ten years in a labor camp: a tribunal convicted him of the crime of "bourgeois humanism."

It was, of course, true that neither the internment camps nor rape were confined to the Soviet sector. The Americans imprisoned thousands of suspected Nazis, often in appalling conditions, for years, and French troops frequently ravaged German women in cities under their control. But in the dying months of the war, Hitler and Goebbels had fanned the flames of national fear by issuing a constant stream of propaganda about the brutality of the Red Army—and from the moment they fought their way onto German soil, the Soviet occupiers fulfilled the worst of these predictions.

Our little family was as vulnerable as any—and possibly more so. My mother and my aunt Eka were young and pretty and our family belonged to the hated bourgeoisie: our home was large, comfortable, and well stocked with food from the farm, but it was also isolated and there were no men in the household. The fear—the dread—of rape was something that hung over our family as the winter wore on. My mother would later remember—one of only a sparse handful of personal feelings she ever shared with me—hiding under the bed whenever she heard rumors that Red Army soldiers were in the area.

But however debilitating the fear, we were, in truth, much better off than most of the population in the Soviet zone. For one thing, our rural retreat gave us a roof over our heads, unlike the vast majority of people in the bombed-out cities. The winter of 1946–1947 was one of the harshest in living memory: temperatures plummeted to minus thirty degrees, and for the millions struggling to exist in the bombed-out basements of their former homes, there was no protection from the biting cold. And since what remained of the rail network after the final, disastrous months of fighting was rapidly being dismantled by the Soviet Army and taken back east as war reparation, there was little coal to be had. Thousands of people simply froze to death.

BUT IT WAS food—or rather, the lack of it—that became, almost overnight, the overriding preoccupation. German ration cards, issued by the now-dismantled Nazi state, were no longer valid; whatever provisions had previously been available—and that was not much by the end of the war—were now being claimed by SMAD to feed the Red Army. In cities across the country, hunger joined fear as the measure of existence.

In the areas under Moscow's control, new rationing measures were introduced. The Russians created a new five-tier system: the highest level was reserved—bizarrely—for intellectuals and artists;

the next level down was assigned to the women—*Trümmerfrauen*, as they were called—who worked in chain gangs, tearing down and clearing semiderelict buildings, often with nothing more than their bare hands. This was much more valuable than the official wages of twelve Reichsmarks they received for cleaning up every thousand bricks. Hard physical labor was the only way to survive, and in the ruins of the nation, Germany's women dug for the salvation of their families.

The levels of rationing below this fell incrementally and dramatically. The lowest card, nicknamed the *Friedhofskarte* (literally meaning "cemetery ticket") was issued to those who performed no useful function in the eyes of our Soviet masters: housewives who did no work, and the elderly.

TWO NEW WORDS joined the growing lexicon of postwar lives that winter. The first was *Fringsen*; it emerged after the Catholic cardinal of Cologne, Josef Frings, gave his formal blessing to what many of his flock were already doing—stealing in order to survive. Crime rose dramatically; in addition to the uncountable (and generally uncounted) tally of thefts and rapes by Red Army soldiers, Germans under Soviet occupation began preying on each other. Berlin alone averaged 240 robberies and five murders every day.

But if urban crime was another source of shame and ongoing fear for the von Oelhafens, for those living in the relative security of rural Mecklenburg, the second new word had an even more powerful meaning. *Hamstern* was that word, and while it meant, quite literally, "to hamster," in practice it referred to a constant procession of city dwellers to and from the countryside, desperate to trade their few remaining possessions for the food we had in relative abundance.

This then, was the reality of *Stunde Null*: an existence defined by three constant companions: fear—especially of the Red Army and of its determination to exact revenge on German civilians for Hitler's war—hunger, and cold. This, then, was Germany, my country and my life on my fourth birthday. These were our reward for the triumphs of the glorious Reich.

There was worse—much worse—in store. Throughout 1946, as relations between the occupying powers worsened, Moscow's intentions toward those under its rule in SMAD became ever starker. As well as stripping the zone of wealth and food, it began the process of removing the one flickering hope we had enjoyed when the war ended: freedom.

The boundaries between the four zones now became increasingly less passable. An "inner German border"—as SMAD termed it—had been established around the Soviet-held territory in July 1945, but since then it had been sporadically (and far from rigorously) policed. Although anyone wanting to move between the Soviet sector and the other Allied occupation zones officially needed an *Interzonenpass*, at least one and a half million Germans were able to flee into the American or British zones. Now that began to change.

In the summer of 1947—as, under Moscow's direction, preparations were made for the eventual transformation of SMAD into the new Communist-ruled German Democratic Republic—new contingents of Soviet soldiers were assigned to the official border checkpoints. Unofficial crossing places would soon be blocked by newly dug ditches and barbed-wire barricades. The Cold War was beginning, and in Bandekow our little family was growing up on the wrong side of the coming Iron Curtain. In the summer of 1947 my parents— separated by a thousand kilometers as well as by the unbridgeable emotional ditches of a broken marriage—made a remarkable joint decision. It was time to escape.

# THREE

---

# Escape

---

*Ingrid is very brave and overcomes the strenuous walk without complaining.*

GISELA VON OELHAFEN'S JOURNAL,
*June 1947*

M Y MOTHER KEPT a journal.
Unknown to me—she never told me about it, even when
I was an adult—she jotted down the barest of details of my early years
across a sparse handful of pages. This slim, black, leather-bound notebook contains all I know about my first eight years of life.

It begins with a small black-and-white photo of me, barefoot
and in little shorts, captioned: *Bandekow—Ingrid, Summer 1944.*
Stuck in between the pages is an envelope dated June 4, 1944, and
containing—according to my mother's note—a few strands of my
hair. But if that seems like the start of a conventional diary, the sort
any loving mother might keep as a record of her daughter's childhood,
the rest of it soon belies that impression. For one thing, there are very
few entries—no more than four of five for each of the five years my
mother troubled to write in it. And then there is the curious nature of
the terse entries themselves. They are all in the third person: throughout, Gisela refers to herself as *Mutti*—the German colloquial word
for "Mommy"—never "I."

Perhaps she did this so that it would be easier for me to read: this sort of third-person journal was, I have since gathered, not uncommon in Germany of the later war years. But then, since she never showed it to me—much less even told me about it—this benign explanation doesn't seem to make much sense. Instead, the curiously detached writing style seems somehow to emphasize the difficulty my mother found in living up to a maternal stereotype and is evidence of the distance I always felt between us.

Still, the journal does give me some idea of what sort of child I was. The entry for my birthday on November 11, 1944, reads: *"Today Ingrid is three years old. At her age she is not tall, but she thrives and prospers wonderfully and has a healthy constitution. She has a strong will and a disposition to violent temper. Her character is calm and persistent. She does not pay attention to people she does not know: at that point her little ego takes center stage and claims a little too much of her small world."*

The next item—dated a month afterward—seems to hint at a desire on my part to win my mother's affections. For reasons undisclosed, I was left alone with Dietmar at lunchtime; when my mother returned she noted that *"Ingrid—with a serious face—was very busy feeding her brother just as Mommy always does."*

IF THE DIARY is any guide, I appear not to have succeeded. Throughout the twelve months of 1945, my mother managed to put pen to paper on only five occasions—two to record the effect of measles on me, one noting the happy news that I was no longer afraid of our family dog, and two more in which my slowness to speak—*"She doesn't make complete sentences, her maximum is three or four words"*—

is observed and preserved. There was a very good reason why I was slow to get my childish tongue around German words; one that, had she thought about it, my mother would have known perfectly well. But there is no mention of this in the pages of the notebook.

Nor does she dwell on what must have been a traumatic period in my life the following year. In the summer, my mother laconically recorded that I (and presumably Dietmar) had been sent away to a children's home, more than 250 kilometers away at Lobetal, near Berlin. How did we get there? I do not know, for my mother's diary is silent on this, as it is on so much else. All that she wrote was that *"Mommy is ill—meanwhile Ingrid lives from August 5th to November 1st in a children's home in Lobetal. There she suffers from mumps—but not too badly."*

MY MOTHER'S ILLNESS—OR so I learned decades later—was in fact a nervous breakdown. Perhaps it was the collapse of her marriage and the burden of looking after two small children. Perhaps it was the strain of living under Soviet occupation, the constant fear of arrest or—worse—rape by the Red Army. Perhaps, too, she was afraid of what could happen if the Soviet administration discovered that I didn't have a birth certificate and that the only documents relating to me were issued by a Nazi organization. Certainly, the first entry in the notebook for 1947 shows that she had made up her mind to escape—and that she had enlisted my father—still estranged from her—in her highly dangerous plans. *"May 1, 1947. Daddy takes both children to the children's home in Lobetal. Mommy wants to cross the border illegally."*

I cannot pretend that I was ever close to my mother, nor can I claim to have ever really felt from her the sort of love that a child should take for granted from a parent. Gisela also plainly knew this; another terse diary entry in my mother's handwriting noted that I was always much fonder of my grandmother than of her. *"Granny is loved over all others, often more than Mommy. She gets on with the children very well."* But even so, I have to acknowledge that the decision to make a bid for freedom was immensely brave.

THE BORDER BETWEEN what would, less than two years later, become the "German Democratic Republic" and the British zone of occupied Germany was both political and physical. It was, of course, forbidden to leave the Soviet zone without a special permit—and, as my mother's scheme to cross the frontier illegally implied, these were far from easy to obtain. Even writing the idea in her diary could—had it been discovered—have led to interrogation, imprisonment in the Silence Camps, or worse.

In addition to this, the journey to the border would have been as arduous and complicated as it was dangerous. Bandekow might have been less than fifteen kilometers as the crow flies from the Elbe River, which marked out much of the boundary with the British zone, but even had we possessed the means of making that journey, there was no way of getting across it. My mother had already made a secret trial run and must have discovered that the nearest bridges at Lauenburg and Dömitz had been blown up by the retreating German Army in 1945. The nearest bridge left intact was 150 kilometers farther south at Magdeburg.

With the country's railways still in chaos—and with private cars (let alone the gas to run them) a rarity—getting to Magdeburg would have been a challenge for a healthy adult, traveling alone. My mother was evidently far from well—and she would have two very young children to drag with her every step of the way. It must have been a daunting prospect.

Encumbered by Dietmar and me, she would not be able to carry anything with her: the three of us would make the trek in whatever clothes we had and—if successful—would arrive in the safety of British territory with nothing more than what we stood up in.

The near impossibility of simply getting from one place to another in 1947 is clear from the convoluted escape route my mother carefully wrote down in the diary. Traced now on a map, the first part of the journey took us east, not west—ever deeper into the Soviet zone and away from the sanctuary we sought.

We began on June 30, traveling—I think—by horse and cart, twenty-five kilometers to the little town of Lübtheen. Here my mother found a hotel to put us up for the night and in which we could await the arrival of her co-conspirator the next morning.

I have no idea how my father managed to obtain papers to cross from the American zone into Soviet-controlled territory; nor can I understand from where he obtained the car into which the four of us crowded that morning. All I know is that the thirty-kilometer journey, eastward to the city of Ludwigslust, would be the last hours we ever spent as a family.

THE REASON FOR heading so far east was waiting for us in the station at Ludwigslust. Both the platform itself and the train that would take us back—westward at last—to Magdeburg must have been very crowded. That summer more than ten million refugees and released prisoners of war were on the move; many were, like us, desperately trying to find a route out of the Soviet zone. Once again, I have no way of knowing how we obtained what must have been precious train tickets; my mother's diary recorded only that my father had to push Dietmar and me into her arms through the train window. Likewise, she makes no mention of the fact that he did not make the journey with us, staying behind on the platform and (so I like to imagine) waving a lonely and fearful farewell to his wife and children.

Magdeburg was more than 150 kilometers south, and the train journey took all day. When we finally arrived it was evening and we must have been both tired and hungry. Finding food would not be an easy task; Magdeburg had been heavily bombed in 1945, and by the time we arrived it was still a city of ruins and ruination. And although it was in the Soviet zone, our Soviet-issued ration cards would not have been valid. Alone with two small children in a strange and devastated city, my mother took the only available option: she found a black-market trader and handed over sixty marks for a few pieces of bread.

THERE IS NO information in my mother's diary about where we stayed that night. In the chaos that was Magdeburg it seems unlikely that we would have found a hotel; the notebook simply records that we stayed there all the next day, changing accommodations in the evening to be closer to the next stage of our path to freedom.

We had, first, to get a train out of Magdeburg, heading north to the village of Gehrendorf. Here, the little river Aller was the boundary between east and west. On the other side was the hamlet of Bahrdorf, safely inside the British zone. All that lay between us and sanctuary were the slowly running waters of the Aller.

There were, however, no boats and no bridges; the only way across was to wade. And so that was what we did.

How long did it take? It cannot have been too long, for the Aller is not wide at the best of times, and in the height of summer would have been quite shallow. Nonetheless, what would have been short work for a healthy adult on her own must have been much more challenging a task for a fraught young woman trailing two very young children in the heat of a midsummer's day. Did she constantly look over her shoulder, hoping not to be seen by Red Army border guards and praying that neither Dietmar nor I would cry out and give our perilous position away?

All I know for sure is what my mother later set down in her notebook: *"The temperature is very high. Ingrid is very brave and overcomes the strenuous walk without complaining."*

Finally we gained the sanctuary of the other side. We crawled up the bank, and after a long trek through no-man's-land we reached the British zone of occupation. We had escaped. We were free.

My mother could not have known it—though, given the urgency and determination that emerge from her succinct account of our flight from east to west, she must have sensed the Iron Curtain beginning to fall—but we had made our getaway just in time. By September 1947, the frontiers between the Soviet zone and those of its former Western allies were closely guarded by a new influx of NKVD troops; it would not be long before orders were given to shoot would-be escapers on sight.

What did freedom look like to Gisela von Oelhafen that summer's evening? What did it mean to her to have reached safety after two years under Soviet occupation, and to have delivered her children from the threat of Moscow's iron rule? I wish I could ask her now.

A DAY'S HARD—but safe—traveling later, we arrived in Wünsdorf, a little town just west of Hanover and the penultimate stop on my mother's journey to her family's home in Hamburg. I say my mother's journey quite deliberately because she would make the last leg of her trek alone. Her diary entry—terse and glacial as ever—recorded the very different fate allocated to Dietmar and me: *"July 4th: To Loccum, children's home."*

She had brought Dietmar and me out of the Soviet zone and into the less dangerous territory of the British sector. But that is as far as her maternal protection extended. No sooner had she spirited us to safety than she sent us away to be looked after by others.

And so my second night of freedom ended in the surroundings of a home for unwanted children. I would spend the next six years—lonely and isolated—in the care of the church. In fact, my new life began exactly as the old life had ended: cold and frightened.

# FOUR

# Homes

*Dear Mommy, please take me home forever. I'm long-ing for you and granny and Aunt Eka.*

LETTER TO MY MOTHER FROM
THE CHILDREN'S HOME

M Y FIRST REAL memory is of an orange.
I have snatches of other, possibly earlier recollections—lying, cold, under a blanket on the floor of a train; a line of camp beds in a long room and a rat running over my feet—but the first actual memory I know to be true is of the orange.

I am at a long wooden dining table in a big room. There are a lot of people, grown-ups and children. I know that many of the adults are homeless men and women who have been invited here for the day; the children, though, live in this building. Each of us is given a plate with fruit on it, including a single orange as a special treat.

I know where and when this memory comes from. The year was 1947 and I was almost six years old. The room with the long table is in the children's home to which Dietmar and I were dispatched. It was Christmas Day.

The home was run by the Protestant church and was called Nothelfer, which, literally translated, means "help us in affliction." There were sixty-five boys and girls living there, all under the age of ten.

Some were displaced persons—children who had lost their parents during the war or in the chaotic mass migrations of the immediate postwar months. Dietmar and I were different: we had two living parents who knew where we were but who, for reasons best known to themselves, had sent us to be cared for by others.

We were physically as well as psychologically isolated. Nothelfer was on Langeoog, a small island in the North Sea ten kilometers from the coast of mainland Germany and two hundred from Hamburg. I don't think my parents had intended to send us so far away; when we first arrived in July it had been situated near Hanover. But at some point in the subsequent five months those premises were closed and we were moved up to Langeoog.

Given its location, it was hardly surprising that Nothelfer was cold. I can still feel the wind whipping up sand from the island's long beach, seemingly stripping the skin from my legs and arms. But it was the emotional coldness that cut more deeply. The home was staffed by sisters from a religious order and at times the regime could be harsh; physical punishment was part of our daily routine.

If we were disobedient, if we wet the bed, if we broke the cardinal rule forbidding us the childish pleasure of sliding down the sand dunes, we were spanked. I remember quite clearly a group of dirty and downcast boys and girls being lined up in front of the harshest of the sisters, who would beat our bare bottoms with a stick. Such was our new life in the west.

We would spend the next four years at Nothelfer. From time to time our parents made the journey out to the island to visit us; but their visits were rare and they never came together, always alone. My father had, by then, moved from the American occupied zone into the British sector, and was building himself a new house in the Westphalian spa resort of Bad Salzuflen. Although he and my mother were separated, they had not divorced (and would never do so). Occasionally they spent a little time together—generally when Dietmar and I were allowed out to visit one of them—but my mother had begun to make a new life for herself in Hamburg.

Immediately after sending us to Nothelfer, she had returned to her family's home in the city, a large three-story building in an exclusive neighborhood. Number 39 Blumenstrasse had three floors and a basement, and large gardens that ran down to Rondeelteich—one of the big lakes in the heart of Hamburg where people went boating, sailing, and swimming. There she lived with her mother, my aunt Eka, and a housekeeper-cum-cook.

INITIALLY THEY ALSO shared the house with British army officers who had been billeted there at the end of the war. Their presence was, ostensibly, the reason why we had been sent to the children's home; according to my mother there was not enough room for us all.

Whether or not this was actually true (since the situation didn't change when the soldiers moved out), it did enable her to start a new life, unencumbered by either husband or two small children. She enrolled at a college and began training to become a physiotherapist; once qualified, she turned one of the ground-floor rooms into a surgery where she worked with a growing clientele of patients.

She also took advantage of her essentially single status to find a boyfriend. Neither Dietmar nor I would ever meet this man, but within two years she gave birth to a baby boy, whom she named Hubertus. He was not, I am certain, my father's child, but he was formally registered as a von Oelhafen.

I cannot, in all honesty, say that my father's visits to Langeoog meant a great deal to us. Whether this was because of his age or his stiff and disciplinarian nature I do not know; what I do recall with awful clarity is the heartache of being apart from my mother, and the loss I felt after her occasional trips to see us. I missed her terribly.

Among her effects years later I found a note from one of the kinder sisters who ran the home.

*Highly honored madam,*

*I'd like to add a few sentences to the letter Ingrid has written to you. For the past few weeks I have been worrying about Ingrid. She yearns intensely for her "Mommy." Every day she talks about "Mommy" or asks: do you think I'm allowed once to go to Mommy? I'd like so much to see her. Aunt Emi, do you think that that I would be allowed to leave the island and stay for a short time with Mommy?*

*Ingrid is eating very little and feels miserable. In my opinion, the reason for this calamity is her longing for Mommy.*

*In school Ingrid is one of the best. She is hardworking. In general she is a nice child.*

*I feel committed to inform you about this.*

*Best wishes from Schwester*
[Sister] *Emi*

If my mother replied to this letter, I never found out. I don't remember whether she replied to the letters I wrote to her, and yet she kept at least some of them. Along with Sister Emi's letter I found this undated note, scrawled in my childish hand after an all-too-brief visit to see her.

*Dear Mommy,*

*Thanks a lot for the parcel. I am only writing a little today.*
*Dear Mommy, please take me home forever. I'm longing for*
*you and grandmother and Aunt Eka. I always cry if someone*
*talks about you, or if I think of you. On the trip* [back to
Langeoog] *I couldn't eat. I still have the chocolate and the two*
*Deutschmarks.*

*Please write as fast as possible to the authorities and say that*
*I'm allowed to leave the island soon. Christa* [another girl in the
home] *will leave the island this month or next. But I want to*
*leave this month!*

*Dietmar told me he has got a lot of fruits and sweets.*
*Dietmar teases me a lot and asks: Why didn't you stay in*
*Hamburg? I want so much to leave the island. Dear Mommy,*
*please arrange that I can leave. Christa told me, she had cried*
*too when she had to go away from her parents.*

*Many greetings and kisses from Ingrid. Don't write to Daddy*
*about me having written to you. Dear, dear Mommy, please come*
*and pick me up.*

She never did. And even the sporadic, terse entries in the little
diary she had—apparently—kept for me ceased abruptly in the summer of 1949.

I was ten years old when I finally left Langeoog for good in 1952.
I had passed the exams to go to *Mittelschule*, the intermediary level
of education between elementary and senior schools, and had high
hopes that at last I would be allowed to live with my mother in Hamburg. It was not to be. My father sent for Dietmar and me; we were to
share his new home in Bad Salzuflen.

By this point Hermann von Oelhafen was sixty-eight years old, bitter at the loss of his wife, suffering from poor health, and utterly ill-equipped to look after young children he barely knew. Of the ten years of my life and nine years of Dietmar's, he had lived with us for a matter of months at most. It was surely a little too late to start being a father.

I think I know now why Hermann brought us to Bad Salzuflen. I think my father still loved Gisela and he hoped our presence there might somehow draw her back to him; that despite her evident love affair with another man—and their child—Dietmar and I would be the glue that mended their broken marriage.

In this, as in much else, he was to be disappointed. My mother came occasionally to visit us (a spare bedroom in the smart, if far from grand house on Akazienstrasse was maintained for her exclusive use) but there was never any question of reconciliation.

From the moment we arrived, life in Bad Salzuflen was horrible. Even as a young child, Dietmar was spirited and difficult, though not particularly naughty. Today he might have been diagnosed with ADHD; certainly he and Hermann fought a battle of wills. He was routinely late coming home from school—even though he never seemed to want to learn there—and Hermann, who was hot-tempered at the best of times, had no understanding or patience for this irritating little boy. Very soon he began to beat Dietmar.

It was frightening to watch; on one occasion he physically threw him across the room. And yet somehow Dietmar wasn't frightened of him. I, by contrast, was terrified; even though my father never hit me, I lived in fear of his temper. I began to rely on Dietmar to ask Hermann's permission to do even the smallest things. One day we wanted to go swimming but I didn't dare ask. Dietmar immediately went in my place, and permission was granted, but it didn't change anything for me. I was still too scared to speak to my father.

And then Dietmar was taken away.

Someone—presumably the children's welfare department of the local government—decided that since Hermann did not live with his wife and that there was therefore no mother in our house, Dietmar could no longer live with us.

There were a number of odd aspects to this decision. For a start it only applied to Dietmar; although he was less than a year older than me, the authorities did not appear to believe I had to be removed from my father's care. Officially the reason for this discrepancy was that I was to be looked after by the middle-aged couple who lived with us as Hermann's cook-cum-housekeeper and general handyman. But no one explained why the paid-for care of Emmi and Karl Harte was good enough for me yet insufficient for Dietmar.

More puzzling still was the revelation that Dietmar had family— a completely different family from ours—living in Munich. Had I been older I would, of course, have realized that the nine months between his birthday and mine meant that we could not have the same mother. But even if I had been old enough to understand this most elementary fact of life, I would not have grasped the fact that the little boy I had always called my brother had, in fact, been fostered by my parents.

And so it emerged that Dietmar had an uncle, an aunt, and a sister—blood relatives all—who had, presumably, been looking for him. I don't remember anyone explaining how he had originally come to live with us instead of them; one day he was simply taken away from Bad Salzuflen. As it turned out, he never rejoined his long-lost family: instead, they placed him in the care of another children's home. I was now on my own (save for the Hartes) in my father's house and, if my letters to Gisela are anything to go by, absolutely terrified.

June 22, 1952

*Dear Mommy!*

*Please send me some envelopes and stamps. Dear Mommy, please pick me up this week and bring me to Hamburg, I'm not able to stay longer with Daddy. I must tell you that my fear of him is greater than before. He told me off once because I've cried about you. Now I cry every day.*

*Dear Mommy, please pick me up immediately, I cannot stand it here with Daddy any longer. Or come and stay here forever. But "Uncle Harte" says you are afraid of Daddy too. Dear Mommy, perhaps you can send the stamps to "Uncle Harte," but don't tell Daddy that I've written to you.*

*Mommy, we can organize it this way: You come and pick me up forever and explain to Daddy you had written to Munich* [to the child welfare department] *to ask whether they would allow me to stay with you. You* [explain that you] *didn't bring the letter with you, but promise to send it when we get back to Hamburg.*

*And in Hamburg we'll write a letter on typewriter and send it to Daddy and pretend it has come from Munich. I'd like so much to come to you just this week, please pick me up quickly. Today I cried again because I have been thinking of you. I'm not in the mood to play because you are not here. Please pick me up at the 25th of June. Greetings and kisses from Ingrid. Please pick me up the 25th. Please, please dear Mommy.*

These pleas went unheeded. Although my mother continued to come for short visits, she never took me home with her. Whether this was because my father forbade it or because she didn't want me to live with her, the outcome was the same: I was effectively imprisoned in the house in Bad Salzuflen with an increasingly bitter and parsimonious old man.

Even as an eleven-year-old I was aware that my father was less well off than my mother. He received a state pension from the new West German government; reward for his years serving both the Kaiser and the Reich as an officer in the army.

But this did not, for example, seem to be sufficient to pay the price of a daily newspaper to be delivered. Instead he would make the journey into town, where he would stand outside the newspaper offices and read the morning's edition, which was always pasted up in the window. Occasionally I was permitted to go with him.

Hermann's health was deteriorating. He had suffered from epilepsy for many years (a condition he had apparently concealed from Gisela when asking her to marry him). Now it became increasingly severe.

Although I never saw him have a full-blown grand mal fit, when a seizure took him he became "absent"—completely lost within himself. There was no way to communicate with him, and his behavior was strange and frightening. Often he picked up a knife and waved it around wildly. Once, he was hospitalized, and while he was away, Frau Harte was more generous than he was with the marmalade for my breakfast. When Hermann came home again he saw how much had been used from the jar and became angry. I was punished for my evident greed by being denied marmalade for a week.

School became my refuge. I had friends whose parents, perhaps seeing how unhappy I was at home, were kind and loving toward me. I loved spending time with them, wishing I could be part of a real family, too. And then, when I was eleven, I discovered that I was not who I thought I was.

I woke up one morning and found that I couldn't open my eyes. My father took me to the doctor's office.

We sat in the reception area, waiting for my turn. When the doctor called out the name, "Erika Matko," my father stood up and led me into the consulting room. He handed over my health insurance card and I saw that it, too, had the name Erika Matko printed on it.

I had no idea why I was being called by a different name. But I didn't dare say anything to the doctor or my father; I was still too frightened of him to question anything. At the end of the consultation I was prescribed a course of sun lamps—a common enough treatment in those days for vitamin deficiency (most likely a problem dating back to my years in the children's home at Langeoog)—and we went back home. Nothing was said about the odd business of the different name, but I had not forgotten.

Shortly after that I had a conversation with Frau Harte. Every Friday it was our routine to clean the house together, and I could talk freely to her about whatever I had on my mind. It was the closest thing I had to a normal relationship with an adult. As we were polishing I asked if she knew why my name was written down as Erika Matko.

EMMI TOLD ME that Hermann and Gisela were not my biological parents. She said that when I was a baby they had fostered me, just like Dietmar, and that my original name was Erika Matko. Emmi wasn't embarrassed to tell me that I had been fostered. The war had fractured so many families and left so many children without parents that our situation was far from unusual.

I don't recall being upset at discovering the truth about myself. I was not close to Hermann and I think that I processed the information by deciding that it explained his coldness toward me, and why I was not allowed to live with Gisela.

But of course I wondered where I had come from. I assumed that my real parents were German—it never occurred to me to think otherwise—and I speculated about what had happened to them. Perhaps they had been in prison; maybe they had died in the war. Emmi said she had wondered whether I was originally Jewish because of my prominent nose. But although my father had told her that I was a foster child, she didn't know any more than that. Everything else was just speculation.

OF COURSE I never said anything to Hermann. Nor, the next time Gisela came to visit, did I ask her about it. But Hermann must have told her about the visit to the doctor's office and I assume she felt she had to say something. She started to tell me that I was fostered and how she had fetched me from a children's home, but I quickly cut her off, saying "I know." I don't really know why I stopped her; perhaps it was my childish way of showing her that it was all too late, that I was hurt that she had kept the truth from me. The subject was never mentioned again.

The one person I would have liked to talk to was Dietmar. We had been close in the children's home and in the few months we had spent together in Hermann's house. But by then he had been taken away and I had no way to contact him. I didn't even have an address that I could write to.

Life continued as before. Every morning I went to school—where I was registered and known as Ingrid von Oelhafen—and returned in the afternoon to the house in Bad Salzuflen I shared with the man I now knew was not my biological father and of whom I was still very afraid.

OVER THE NEXT two years Hermann's health continued to deteriorate and he was often still in bed when I left for school. I would go into his room to wish him good morning, but in truth this was no more than living up to my duties as a good daughter.

Then, one morning in April 1954, toward the end of the spring term and with the long summer holidays approaching, I said good-bye to him as usual. I noticed that he seemed a little disoriented when I left, but I didn't say anything to Emmi and Karl Harte because I assumed it was just another symptom of his illness. But when I came back from school he was in a very bad way; it was clear he had had a stroke. My father—my foster father, as I now knew him to be—was taken to the hospital and died two weeks later.

I have to admit that I was not sad. I felt happy to be free of him and his harsh, unforgiving ways. And I assumed that at long last I would be allowed to live with Gisela in Hamburg. What did hurt me was Emmi and Karl's reaction; they criticized me severely for not telling them about Hermann's condition that morning.

My high hopes for a new life with my mother—I still thought of her as "Mommy" then, even though I knew I wasn't her "real" child— were not to be; or not immediately, at least. Gisela was too busy with her thriving physiotherapy practice and her five-year-old son, Hubertus.

For six long months I continued living in Hermann's home with the Hartes looking after me. It was not until nearly October 1954 that I was finally sent to Hamburg. And by then, the strange story of Erika Matko and my true identity seemed to have been forgotten.

# FIVE

# Identity

*The lost identity of individual children is the Social Problem of the day on the continent of Europe.*

INTERNATIONAL REFUGEE ORGANIZATION
INTERNAL MEMORANDUM,
*May 1949*

WHEN I WAS fifteen years old I saw my face on a poster in the street.

A decade after the end of the war, and seven years after the formation of our new federal republic, Germany was still a nation of displaced and unclaimed children. United Nations agencies had spent those years searching across Europe for close to two million missing boys and girls, separated from their parents by bombings, military service, evacuation, deportation, forced labor, ethnic cleansing, or murder. By 1956 it had traced just 343,000 of them.

The Red Cross had decided that one way to search for children who may have been brought to Germany during the war was to post photos of them as they were then in newspaper advertising columns. Underneath these lists of faces and names ran the headline: WHO KNOWS OUR PARENTS AND OUR ORIGINS? They also pasted up large posters on columns and lampposts on streets across West Germany. It was from one of these, in the center of Hamburg, that my younger face peered back at me.

It was, to say the least, a shock. I had no idea that anyone was looking for me or how they would have obtained my photograph. I had to presume that Gisela had given it to the authorities, but no one had said anything about it to me.

By that point I had been living in the house on Blumenstrasse in Hamburg for two years. Two years during which my dreams of a happy family life had proved to be no more than an unrealistic and childish fantasy. I had spent half of my young life longing to be with my mother, aching to feel loved and looked after. By the time I saw my photograph on the poster, reality had set in—and set me in my ways.

I knew, of course, that Gisela was not my real mother, that I was a foster child, a cuckoo somehow brought into her nest, but I still had no idea when—much less how or why—she and Hermann had taken me in, and I had pushed the whole business to the back of my mind. I wanted so much to cling to the belief that I belonged to Gisela and her family.

What I couldn't hide from, though, was the way Gisela treated me. She was not cruel—I could never call her that. But she was noticeably cold—emotionally and physically—toward me.

This was in stark contrast to her other relationships. Professionally, she was an extremely successful physiotherapist; her patients clearly loved her, and she returned their affection. With her own relatives, too, she was warm: to her mother and her sister Eka (Aunt Eka, to whom I increasingly turned for love and understanding), and toward her son. Hubertus was eight years younger than me, a very good-looking boy, who—unlike me at his age—could speak well and fluently. It might have been easy not to like him: he was, after all, Gisela's natural child and had been living in the house in Hamburg throughout the six-month delay before I was allowed to go there. But although I resented the fact that Gisela seemed able to show love to almost anyone but me, I had come to care very much for Hubertus and we had a strong bond between us.

But this was a rare glimpse of light. Teenage years are always difficult, especially, I think, for girls. The crucial years between thirteen and fifteen are generally a time of uncertainty and insecurity, and a time when it is all too easy to be critical of adults. But in Germany in 1956, that developmental confusion was exacerbated by a national crisis.

The Nazis and the war had broken the previously close bonds of German family life just as surely as the bombs and tanks had destroyed the country's houses, bridges, and railways.

In addition to creating a huge population of orphans, Hitler's desperate last-ditch battles had blurred the lines between childhood and adult life by throwing young boys into the doomed fighting.

In the immediate postwar years an army of international psychologists and social workers was called in to address the problems for Germany's next generation. The men and women of the United Nations Refugee Relief Organization (UNRRA) and its successor, the International Refugee Organization (IRO), recognized that many teenagers in the late 1940s and early 1950s were growing up without the emotional security they needed—both individually and as part of an emerging new nation. An internal IRO memorandum in May 1949 highlighted the crisis in stark terms.

*The lost identity of individual children is the Social Problem of the day . . .*

And so, while the American secretary of state, George Marshall, put in place a vast economic aid plan to rebuild Germany's shattered infrastructure and economy (and the rest of Europe), UNRRA and

IRO set to work on what they termed a "psychological Marshall Plan" for its children.

First they had to identify us. Along with the posters, radio announcements instructed those fostering children from other countries to report to their local youth administration office. How did this affect us? I could not have told you then what Gisela did; it would be decades before I learned that she met with the investigators without telling me. But when I came face-to-face with my photo on the poster, I had conflicting emotions.

Of course, I wondered who my real parents were. Perhaps my father had been—like Hermann—an officer in the Wehrmacht who went away to war, leaving me with a mother who either didn't want me, or could not cope alone with a baby. Those were my rational thoughts. But behind them were the sharp pangs of fear and hope. Hope that my biological mother would see the posters, track me down, and take me back. Fear, because I was worried what sort of person this woman would turn out to be if she ever did turn up. Perhaps she would be worse than Gisela; maybe she wouldn't even like me. But these were only flickering emotions and in the end it was easier to snuff them out than to dwell on them. Even though I wasn't happy and I knew that the von Oelhafens and the Andersens were not my blood relatives, I clung to the belief that in some way I belonged to them.

Does it sound odd that the mystery of who I was and where I had come from was never discussed? Perhaps. At the time it was simple: I did not have enough of a relationship with Gisela to ask her difficult questions. It would be a long time before I understood that she might well have had very good reasons for wanting to leave the past alone and undisturbed.

Whatever the reason, the subject was never broached; to all intents and purposes I was Ingrid von Oelhafen, the name under which I was registered at school. I did not have one of the new identity cards, issued by the federal government from 1951 onward, but since I was a child, no one thought I would need one until I reached the legal age of majority: twenty-one in those days.

As it turned out, the problem of my identity surfaced sooner than expected. I wasn't doing well at school: academic work—particularly math—was not my strong point. I had decided that I wanted a career as either a children's nurse or a vet, but Gisela had other ideas. Although she sent me for tests that showed that I had enough potential to take the German equivalent of A levels, the British exams used to qualify for university, Gisela wanted me to earn money as soon as possible. And so it was arranged that I would leave school at the age of sixteen.

I was unhappy about this decision and I was convinced that behind everything was the fact that I was a foster child. But I didn't ask Gisela to change her mind. In fact I made a point of never really asking her for anything because I was afraid she would refuse. Looking back, I think this was a sort of self-protection stemming from the time when I had pleaded in vain with her to take me away from Hermann's house.

Gisela's plan was for me to train as a physiotherapist, with a view of going to work in her practice at some point. But I couldn't begin my college course in physiotherapy for another two years. I still have no idea why I was pulled out of school so early, but as a stopgap measure, I was sent off to live with the son of a friend of Gisela's mother who owned a farm near Lake Constance on the border between Germany, Switzerland, and Austria.

Here I was supposed to learn household management. The farm was in a village called Heiligenhaus; it was remote and tiny, with only three or four houses nearby. For the first four weeks I cried every night because I was so homesick. Gradually, though, I settled in. The farmer had six daughters and the youngest two, aged twelve and fourteen, became good friends of mine. The farmer's wife was kind and warm, just as I supposed a mother should be. I stayed with them eleven months, and though I didn't really learn any household or cooking skills—my duties were mostly washing up and helping in the fields— they were very good to me, and inadvertently forced Gisela to do something about my lack of official documentation.

At some point during my stay, the family wanted to go on holiday to Switzerland. But I had no papers—no ID card, no passport, not even so much as a birth certificate—which would be needed to cross the border. The only documentation that anyone seemed to have for me was my state health insurance certificate, and that was in the name of the mysterious Erika Matko.

In 1957 children could be included on their parents' documents. Faced with the prospect of leaving me behind (or abandoning his holiday plans altogether), the farmer passed me off as one of his own daughters. We crossed and recrossed the border without incident.

But it prompted him to write to Gisela, urging her to sort out my identity documents—if for no other reason than I was shortly to be dispatched to somewhere where border controls were likely to be less relaxed.

There was still almost a year before I was to begin my physiotherapy training. Rather than spending it back in Hamburg, it was arranged that I was to be sent to England to work as an au pair. I would need a passport.

To this day I have no idea how Gisela arranged it. I never saw a passport in my name, and given what was to follow, I'm as sure as can be that I was never issued one. Some form of documentation must have been procured, however, as I was able to make the long journey— alone, again—to a small village in Hertfordshire, thirty miles north of London.

The family I was to live with were evidently wealthy. The father was a banker who traveled into London every day. His wife was much younger and spent most of her time with the family's horses.

Of their four children, two were away at Gordonstoun—the famous boarding school where Prince Charles was a student. The third child, an eight-year-old boy, joined them not long after I arrived, leaving me with only the couple's five-year-old daughter to look after. I spent six months in their grand house and thoroughly enjoyed the experience. The couple treated me very well; I had a lovely bedroom with a private bathroom, and they made me feel like part of their family.

Looking back, I doubt I recognized then the irony of finding in the land of my country's former enemy the emotional warmth I had longed for at home. I was only seventeen and not as aware of history as I have since become. I returned to Hamburg with happy memories.

Completely unknown to me, while I had been away the problem of my identity had once again surfaced, and this time it was urgent. The start date for my physiotherapy course was approaching and the university needed my birth certificate to register me as a student. I assume that Gisela was somehow involved in dealing with this. (It would be many years before I discovered the flurry of correspondence between various local government offices about me—and in those letters the first hints about my origins.) But whatever she told the officials it was not, I think, wholly truthful.

MY NEW BIRTH certificate—dated 1959, the first time my existence was formally registered—was in the name of Erika Matko. It was issued by Standesamt 1 in Berlin, the federal government registry that had been specifically created to issue papers for people who had come (or had been forcibly brought) into Germany mainly from the east and who had no other documentation. And yet, oddly, it recorded my birthplace as St. Sauerbrunn in Austria. It was a record that would, many years later, hamper the search for my true identity.

At the time, regardless of my birth certificate, I continued to insist that I was Ingrid von Oelhafen. That was the name I answered to and the one by which my friends at university came to know me. To the university authorities, however, I was someone else; they had registered me in the name of Erika Matko, and when I graduated three years later, aged twenty-one, that was the name on my degree certificate. When I asked the university to change this to Ingrid von Oelhafen, my request was refused: without any official paperwork to prove that I was Ingrid, the administration insisted that I was Erika.

It was 1962 and I was now an adult, about to enter the world of work (and to pay my taxes and Social Security contributions) for the first time. My first job was in an institute in the Black Forest. I was quite used to being away from home by now; I had not really lived with Gisela for any length of time since I left school. And I found myself thoroughly enjoying my new life away from her and without the complications that had dogged my existence back in Hamburg. It was not to last.

In the last year of my training, shortly before my twenty-first birthday, Gisela had had a serious accident. She had fallen down the stairs and lapsed into a coma, which lasted six months. Even when she eventually woke, she was so severely ill that she remained in the hospital for another year. My grandmother and Aunt Eka had taken charge of her affairs while she was hospitalized, but when it was time for her to be discharged, I was needed. With some regret, I left my job in the Black Forest and returned to Hamburg.

Gisela was then forty-nine years old, still relatively young and the mother of a young boy, but now severely disabled. The fall had left her with brain damage and she was unable to walk. There was no prospect of her retaking the reins of her physiotherapy practice; instead, it was decided that I would have to do so.

It was the last thing I wanted to do. I was uncomfortable about taking over Gisela's business, and I also had to abandon plans to go to America, where I had wanted to study a new technique. I knew, too, that the tangled relationships in the von Oelhafen family would not be easy to manage.

I moved back into my old room in the house on Blumenstrasse. It was a difficult time; my grandmother, Aunt Eka, Hubertus, and I all had to adjust to our new circumstances—and to Gisela's condition. It was particularly difficult for Hubertus to see his mother so disabled, but as she learned to walk in the garden and was even able to share occasional laughter, his unhappiness eased.

The big problem was that Hubertus and Eka didn't understand one another and this often led to arguments. I was caught between them because each sought my support against the other. I hated these situations. Nor were things easy with Gisela. She was, to some extent, like a young child, and my aunt tended to speak to her as a strict teacher would address a recalcitrant pupil. My mother, of course, resented this and became stubborn.

Hubertus and I found it easier to accept her as she was because we were younger. But I often found myself feeling aggrieved; I was made to feel very much like a foster child, with few rights but enormous responsibility. It didn't seem right or fair, but I knew that I had no choice but to get on with the job and make the best of it.

After a while, for the first time in as long as I could remember, my relationship with Gisela improved. We didn't talk much but she lost some of the coldness toward me that had marred my younger years.

I realized, of course, why this was; her disability had softened her, and as she was now increasingly dependent on me, she let me see that I was needed.

In other circumstances or other families, it might have opened the door to an open and frank discussion about my past, and how I came to be fostered by her and Hermann.

But that never happened. We never spoke about Hermann. I think that after his death she, like me (although for very different reasons), felt free of him, and in her case, free of the burden of their failed marriage. Perhaps because they had never divorced, she had felt tied to him and haunted by the need to justify her refusal to live with him.

Or so I suppose now. Gisela never discussed her marriage with me, just as she never talked to me about my origins.

The question of who I really was had not, of course, gone away. In the mid-1960s I decided to take matters into my own hands. Although I called myself Ingrid von Oelhafen, officially I was still Erika Matko. The time had come formally to change my name.

But the process turned out to be more difficult than I had imagined. I discovered that German law required me to seek the permission of the von Oelhafen family. Even if Gisela had been well enough to do this, the regulations did not recognize her as a von Oelhafen. She had married into the name; the law recognized only those who had been born into it as the true owners of its heritage. Once again, the old German belief in the sanctity of blood resurfaced.

IRONICALLY—SINCE HE WAS definitely not Hermann's son—because Hubertus had originally been registered with the authorities in the name of von Oelhafen, he was, in theory, allowed to grant permission. But he was then still legally a child and too young to sign any official documents. I don't know why but Hubertus had an official guardian, a lawyer, and so I had to write to this guardian to plead my case. Eventually he agreed, with one qualification: I was not permitted to call myself Ingrid von Oelhafen, since I wasn't part of the family by blood. Instead I could style myself "Ingrid Matko–von Oelhafen"—a signal to the outside world that I was, in some way, a lesser member of the clan. It was hurtful, but there was nothing to be done. I signed the papers and obtained my new name. The certificate cost one hundred marks.

I needed to apply for a passport around the same time and was alarmed to discover when I did so that the authorities wanted to classify me as "stateless." Apparently the unresolved question of where I had been born, and to whom, was still an obstacle to being recognized as a genuine German citizen. I was stunned. The ruling made me feel worthless, as though I were a nothing, a nobody. Nor could I understand why it should be—after all, I had been paying taxes for more than three years. Worse still, the classification could have meant that I was not allowed to vote in elections and that I would not be able to travel freely abroad. It took many months, and the assistance of a lawyer friend of Eka's, before the government relented and I was issued a passport showing me to be a real German.

I didn't know it then, but had Gisela been less disabled (or had she been honest with me years earlier), she could have given me a document that she had kept hidden away for more than twenty years that would have cut through all the red tape and bureaucracy. But she wasn't honest, and she hadn't been—and it would be another three decades before I found it in a cache of other vital paperwork.

Of those decades there is little to tell that is truly relevant to this story. I spent six years in Gisela's house in Hamburg, running her physiotherapy practice. I wasn't particularly happy with this arrangement; Gisela's clientele was largely made up of the elderly, and my interests lay elsewhere.

On one occasion a three-year-old girl who couldn't walk came to the surgery; much as I wanted to help her, I wasn't qualified to do so. From that moment I knew that I wanted to work with children.

I found out about a course at Innsbruck, in the Austrian Tyrol, to learn a new technique for helping disabled youngsters. It would take me away from Hamburg for ten weeks, and a substitute would be needed to look after Gisela's practice (as I still thought of it) while I was away. Aunt Eka was not happy about my going, but I was determined.

Toward the end of the course, I was offered a job on the staff at the Innsbruck University clinic. I worried about what my aunt would say—and what would happen to Gisela—but in the end I accepted and spent a happy year doing what I loved in a place where I felt comfortable.

It was during my time in Innsbruck that I fell in love. I met a young man who came from Osnabrück—close to Bad Salzuflen, where I had lived with Hermann, and even closer to the house in Hamburg. We began a life together in Osnabrück, albeit in separate apartments.

OUR RELATIONSHIP DIDN'T last. For whatever reason, I did not find—have never found—it easy to maintain adult relationships with men. Whether this has something to do with my childhood I cannot say: I know only that while I like the idea of falling in love, those to whom I have often been attracted don't feel the same way about me, and I never seemed to like those men who did see something in me that appealed to them.

I do not say any of this to elicit your sympathy: I am not, by nature, comfortable with that, and if I have never known the intimacy of married life or had my own children, I have been fortunate always to find and keep good friendships with other women that have sustained me.

And I have known, too, the joy of helping many, many children. In the early 1970s, after years of working in hospitals, I established my own physiotherapy practice dedicated to working with disabled youngsters. From then on I worked six days a week, twelve hours a day, consumed by the need to help them. Every year I traveled across Europe, England, and the United States, attending specialized courses that extended my understanding and developed my skills. It has been a lifelong and rewarding career that has brought me immense happiness.

BUT WHAT OF Gisela, the von Oelhafens, and the Andersens? What of the life I walked away from in Hamburg, the strange mystery of my birth, and the circumstances by which I came to be fostered? Although I remained in touch with the family throughout my adult life—and stayed close to Eka, in particular—I did not return to live with them, nor work again in Gisela's business.

By the time I did—briefly—go back to Hamburg, the walls had come down across Germany and the east.

# SIX

# Walls

*Because she is a child of German stock, on the orders of the Reichsführer she is to be brought up in a German family.*

STURMBANNFÜHRER GÜNTHER TESCH

A T 10:45 P.M. on Thursday, November 9, 1989, the Berlin Wall—
the most visible and entrenched symbol of the Iron Curtain—
began to crumble. I was forty-eight years old; for almost half a century
my life—and that of every German—had been shaped by the division
of our country into east and west.

It had been a bitter partition; its most visible symbol may have
been the wall that divided Berlin, but beyond that, East Germany had
reinforced its borders, imprisoning its population inside a rigid ideological police state. Those who sought to flee, as Gisela had once done
with Dietmar and me, found their way blocked by barbed wire and
checkpoints—and by troops under orders to shoot anyone trying to
make their way to freedom. More than a thousand men, women, and
children had died—had been killed—trying to escape the iron grip of
communism.

And then it was over. After a day of confusion and rumor, the
East German commander of the key border checkpoint in the wall
that divided Berlin opened the gate and ordered his guards to allow

people through. Hundreds of *Ossis*—as those from the East were known—swarmed through to be greeted by West Berliners waiting with flowers and champagne.

Before long, a crowd of *Wessis* climbed on top of the wall, where they were joined by East German youngsters. They danced together, joyously celebrating the new freedom. Within hours television cameras captured images of people using hammers and chisels to chip lumps off the Wall: soon these *Mauerspechte*—literally "wall woodpeckers"—demolished entire lengths of the hated structure, creating several unofficial border crossings.

The speed of events took the governments of both East and West Germany by surprise. Yet, in truth, change had been in the air for months. It had begun in August when Hungary—physically and politically one of the outliers of the eastern bloc Moscow had created—effectively dismantled its physical border with Austria. Within weeks more than thirteen thousand *Ossis* had traveled to Hungary and then into Austria. When the government in Budapest tried to stop the flow, East Germans simply marched into the West German embassy and refused to return home. It was an unprecedented act of civil disobedience from a nation that had, for fifty years, grown used to obeying the orders of its Communist masters: and there was more to come.

Throughout that early autumn mass demonstrations broke out across East Germany. Protesters took to the streets chanting *"Wir wollen raus!"* ("We want out!") and *"Wir sind das Volk!"* ("We are the people!"). Newspapers and television stations began proclaiming the dawn of a peaceful revolution.

By the time Erich Honeker resigned as general secretary of the ruling Socialist Unity Party in October, the movement was plainly unstoppable. Honeker was not merely the head of state; as the man who had been in control of East Germany since the early 1970s, he was seen as the embodiment of the Communist state itself.

Despite the warning signs, the collapse of the physical borders was chaotic and unplanned. In the early afternoon of November 9 a televised press conference in East Berlin first hinted that a limited exodus might be permitted. But after hearing the broadcast, people began gathering at the six checkpoints between East and West Berlin, demanding that border guards immediately open the gates. The soldiers were taken by surprise and overwhelmed by the sheer number of those seeking to cross into the west; they made panicky phone calls demanding new instructions.

It soon became clear that no one in the disintegrating East German government would take personal responsibility for issuing shoot-to-kill orders; as a result, the border guards simply stepped aside and allowed the huge crowds to pass peacefully into the west. At a little before 11 p.m., West German television pronounced the last rites of the German Democratic Republic.

*This is a historic day. East Germany has announced that, starting immediately, its borders are open to everyone. The GDR is opening its borders . . . the gates in the Berlin Wall stand open.*

The opening—and the determined dismantling—of the Berlin Wall was followed inevitably by the abandoning of all checkpoints between East and West Germany. By July 1, 1990, the day the Deutschmark was adopted throughout Germany, all border controls officially ceased to exist. Three months later East Germany was dissolved and absorbed into a new unified republic.

What did all this mean to me? Although I was born in the early years of the war, I was really a child of the fifties and sixties—decades in which West Germany had sought to hide the crimes of the past amid the divisions and troubles of the present. I cannot pretend that the reunification of my country meant any more to me than it meant to most people of my generation; we were simply thankful to have grown up on the "right" side of the Iron Curtain and vaguely reassured that the tide of history had somehow restored the proper and natural order. To be sure there were economic fears; no one seemed quite certain what the cost of creating our new country might be, though there were regular and dire predictions that the German economic miracle—for so long the envy of Europe—would be threatened by the need to support our less developed—and bankrupt—former neighbor.

But such fears were primarily for politicians, less alarming for a physical therapist with her own successful practice living in the security of Lower Saxony.

When reunification happened I was fifty years old. I had never married and my life was comfortable. I was financially secure, had a lovely home, and I was working harder than ever. There were, though, clouds building. And inevitably they centered around Gisela.

My foster mother's disability had worsened as the years had passed and she was now severely handicapped. Tragedy had also struck the family. Hubertus, the handsome little boy I had known as a child, had grown up into an attractive gay man; in the mid-1980s he had been among the first German men to be diagnosed as suffering from the terrifying—and then always fatal—new disease of AIDS. In 1988 it claimed him.

The decision to hire a full-time caregiver to look after Gisela had seemed, at the time, the best way of securing her future. Gisela was well off. Her practice had provided well for her, and both the von Oelhafens and the Andersens had money. But the woman we hired saw an opportunity. Not long after Hubertus's death she took advantage of Gisela's enfeebled mind and persuaded her to move to Gran Canaria, one of the Canary Islands, where, she said, they would benefit from a warmer climate. And so the two of them set up home together, more than three thousand miles away from any of the family.

Worse, her companion worked hard to cut us all off from Gisela and to isolate her completely; none of us was able—or allowed—to contact her.

Only when Gisela developed dementia was I permitted to go and visit her. What I found in Gran Canaria disturbed me greatly; it was apparent that Gisela was entirely dependent on a woman whose chief concern was to extract as much money as possible from her before she died. Something had to be done.

Together with Aunt Eka I petitioned the German Guardianship Court to order that we be allowed to intervene in Gisela's life. At first the court refused to hear our plea, saying I had no right because I was only Gisela's foster daughter, not her biological child. Once again the historic German obsession with blood trumped the obvious and urgent need to protect the vulnerable. But unusually for me—I am not, by nature, forceful—I dug in my heels and said to the judges, "I will sit here until you listen to me. I will stay here in this court until you listen to what I have to say."

Eventually they agreed to hear me. I stood up and told the court that Gisela was being controlled by her caregiver and that this woman had manipulated the relationship to such an extent that she had been named as one of the main beneficiaries in Gisela's will. I begged the court to safeguard her interests. But listening to me was as far as the judges were prepared to go; ultimately, the court declined to intervene.

It was left to Aunt Eka to work out a private compromise settlement that provided some measure of protection for Gisela, although it also meant that the caregiver would eventually get some of the money.

But the damage had been done; Gisela lived on until 2002, but never again would we be a family.

Her exile in Gran Canaria did, however, have one positive outcome. When Aunt Eka and I finally realized that Gisela would never return to Hamburg, we set about clearing out her rooms. Which is how I came to find the diary she had kept of my earliest years.

I will remember forever the moment I laid my hands on it, and the emotion I felt when I read its few handwritten pages. I was so very thankful. I had found something about me and my early life—however little, however sparse, it was the first time I could physically reach out and touch my past. But alongside the joy there was pain, too.

I think, perhaps, I hadn't realized the extent to which I had, for nearly forty years, blocked off my feelings about the mystery of my childhood. As I held the little volume, eagerly devouring Gisela's account, the sense of loss and uncertainty came back to overwhelm me. Why had she not given me this diary? Why had she kept it hidden all these years? How could she not have realized what it would mean to me?

What made this all the more painful was the knowledge that I had only discovered the book because Gisela had—to all intents and purposes—abandoned her family once again. That she was in no state to understand this, and that her caregiver was deliberately exploiting her frailty, did not change the fact that I could not contact her to ask all the questions that the diary prompted.

Perhaps this overpowering sense of loss and hurt explains why I did not look more closely at the other documents I found in Gisela's room. I glanced at them and saw that they seemed to be legal papers about the process by which Gisela and Hermann had fostered me. But rather than pay them the attention I should have, I put them away and devoted myself to my work. It would not be until the twentieth century was about to end that I was reminded of their existence.

One day in the autumn of 1999 I was working as usual at my practice when the phone rang. I assumed the caller would be one of my patients, or perhaps a referral for a new client. But the lady on the phone that morning was neither of these things. She first asked whether I was Ingrid von Oelhafen and then explained that she was from the German Red Cross. I was initially puzzled. Why would the Red Cross be calling me? I had no professional connection with the organization: certainly none of my patients had ever come from there.

Then she asked a question that took me completely by surprise: Would I be interested in looking for my birth parents?

I find it hard to describe the feelings that ran through me in that moment. For so long I had put the questions of who I was and where I had come from to the back of my mind, telling myself that working with disabled children was more important; in truth, though, I think I was really avoiding the issue for fear, perhaps, of what I might find. And so I was surprised that my overriding emotion was one of real excitement; at long last I had the chance to find out about my origins. Perhaps I was now finally ready to face the truth.

Why then? Why was I suddenly able to start the journey into the past after so many decades of not doing so? I have thought about this a great deal and come to the conclusion that it was age that made the difference. I was fifty-eight when I received that phone call, and looking back I realize that the older I became, the more I had wondered about my personal history. I am not alone in this; it is, I think, the human condition to revisit the past as the years slip away. It means more to the old than to the young.

There were practical considerations, too. Whenever I had cause to visit a doctor—something that becomes slightly more frequent with advancing years—I would be asked about the history of diseases in my family. And of course I had to say that I had no idea.

I didn't ask how the Red Cross knew where to find me. Or how they knew that I had a family mystery to solve. I simply said yes, and hoped for the best. I don't honestly know whether I thought that the Red Cross would be able to answer my questions. So much of that conversation passed over me in a blur, but what I do know is that the organization wasn't able to tell me anything; it apparently had no secrets to pass on, no insights to drop into my lap. Instead, I was told to contact an academic historian at the University in Mainz.

I owe an immense debt to Georg Lilienthal. When I sat down to write to him I had no idea who he was—much less how important his role would be in both my story and that of Lebensborn. I simply knew what the Red Cross had told me: he was the person who could set my feet on the path I would need to follow.

I understood that Dr. Lilienthal would be expecting my letter, so I wrote openly and honestly, explaining that I had always wanted to know where I came from but that I had never known how or where to start.

When I had finished and posted the letter I was so excited that I wanted to get in the car and drive to Mainz the next day. But something told me that I should wait; whatever information this man had, he would surely need time to pull it together. And so I resolved to be patient and use the time to search through the documents I had found in Gisela's room.

I felt tantalizingly close to discovering the story of how I came to be fostered by Gisela and Hermann, and it was frustrating to still be in the dark. But I had waited fifty years before embarking on this quest; a few more weeks wouldn't kill me.

I dug out the box of Gisela's papers. I had not even looked at them in the years since I found them while clearing out her room, and even then the diary with its precious record of my first few years of life had claimed all my attention. Now I began to look closely at the sheaf of fading documents that had been kept with it.

The first was a small and slightly dog-eared pink slip. It was a vaccination certificate, dated January 19, 1944, and signed at Kohren-Sahlis, near Leipzig: it showed that Erika Matko, born on November 11, 1941, in a town called St. Sauerbrunn, had been inoculated against smallpox.

The date was significant: January 1944 was several months before Gisela and Hermann began fostering me. But other than indicating that the signatory was a doctor, nothing else on the form showed where the vaccination had taken place, or at whose request. What organization had been based at Kohren-Sahlis? And, for that matter, where *was* St. Sauerbrunn?

There was a second certificate that listed further vaccinations recorded. On the reverse side of it was an official stamp that seemed to offer a partial answer to those questions: it read, *Lebensborn Heim Sonnenwiese Kohren-Sahlis.*

*Heim* meant a children's home; that much I knew from my earliest days and it would certainly fit with Hermann and Gisela fostering me. But what was *Lebensborn*? I had never heard the word, but it seemed certain that it had some medical involvement with Erika Matko and therefore must have played a role in the mystery of my past.

The next document was even more puzzling. Dated August 4, 1944, it seemed to be a kind of contract-cum-receipt for my foster parents.

*The family Hermann von Oelhafen, of Gentz Strasse 5, Munich, has on June 3, 1944, taken into their home the ethnic German girl Erika Matkow* [sic], *born 11 November 1941. Because she is a child of German stock, on the orders of the Reichsführer she is to be brought up in a German family.*

*There will be no provision for the maintenance of the child from either side: the child herself has no assets or revenue. The foster parents alone shall be responsible for her support.*

The certificate had apparently been issued in Steinhöring. This, I knew, was a small village not far from Munich; but there was no other information about the organization itself. The only clue was a strange-sounding heading at the top of the paper, almost obscured by tears, hole punches, and the passage of time: *Der Reichskommissar für die Festigung deutschen Volkstums, Stabshauptamt L.*

I had no idea what this could be; a little research revealed it to have been the Office of the Reichs Commissioner for Strengthening German Nationhood—a Nazi organization. But what exactly that did was not immediately clear.

The one thing that stood out was the signature at the bottom of the document: a Dr. Tesch, who described himself as a *Sturmbannführer*. Anyone who had grown up in Germany after the war knew that word: it was a paramilitary rank in the Third Reich, equivalent to a major in the regular army, but it was almost exclusively reserved for use by members of the SS. Why would an officer in Heinrich Himmler's reviled Death's-Head* organization have had anything to do with my foster care? I looked again at the certificate; it said that I had been handed over to a German family "on the orders of the *Reichsführer.*" That was Himmler again; what role could Hitler's second in command, the most feared man in Nazi Germany, have played in my childhood?

---

* The SS cap badge was a death's-head (skull and crossbones): because of this and their role in administering the death camps, they were known as SS Totenkopfverbände—literally, Death's Head units or regiments.

I was desperate to ask Gisela what all this meant—and, indeed, why she had kept these documents from me for so many years. But Gisela was in Gran Canaria and, by this stage, in the last throes of her dementia. I knew I would get no help from her.

A WEEK HAD now passed since I sent Georg Lilienthal my letter. I wondered if he was away from his office or whether for some reason he was unwilling to share with me what the Red Cross said he knew— or at least suspected—about my history. In the interim, I decided to begin my own investigations. I wrote to the German state archives— the Bundesarchiv—and ask if they held any documents bearing my name or that of Erika Matko.

I assumed—naively—that the Bundesarchiv would reply quickly; after all, how difficult could it be, in this age of computerized data-bases, to run a simple check on my names? I was about to discover one of the paradoxes of the new Germany: while the new state was com-mitted to uncovering the terrible sins committed by the rulers of the old East German state, and zealous in rooting out of public life those who had been involved with its secret police, the Stasi, it was much less willing to face up to all the crimes committed by Hitler's Thou-sand Year Reich.

In part this was a legacy of the early postwar years. Konrad Ade-nauer, the first chancellor of West Germany, had vehemently opposed much of the Allied Powers' attempts at denazification, and had worked for the release of the Nazi war criminals convicted at the Nuremberg trials. He had even appointed, as his right-hand man in government, Hans Globke—a politician who had once drafted anti-Semitic laws for Hitler in 1938.

From the outset, no one had wanted to look too closely at the past, and for all its pride as the driving force of the European Union, by the end of the century Germany still had skeletons in its historical closet—skeletons it was neither ready nor willing to rattle.

The Berlin Wall had not been the only barrier to separate Germany from itself. If the nation was now reunited, our collective memory was still decidedly patchy. Over the coming months I would discover that anything relating to the mysterious Lebensborn program seemed to spark repeated bouts of amnesia. I would find that very little information had been published about it, and what information was available suggested a story of national shame and a legacy still shrouded in secrecy.

As I WAITED for Georg Lilienthal and the Bundesarchiv to write back to me I thought back to the telephone call from the Red Cross. The woman had seemed reluctant to tell me anything. Had she been trying to warn me about the problems I would face when she asked me if I really wanted to investigate my past? Perhaps; but however difficult the task might be, I was determined to try. I did not realize then, as I began my personal quest, that I would also be embarking on a painful journey into Germany's troubled history—as well as that of a country it had once invaded and plundered.

# SEVEN

# Source of Life

*The eternal law of nature to keep the race pure is the legacy that the National Socialist movement has bestowed upon the German people for all time.*

NAZI PROPAGANDA FILM,

*1935*

THERE WAS NO such place as St. Sauerbrunn.

With little else to go on, I had decided to go back to the very first record of my existence: the little pink slip of paper showing that I had been vaccinated against scarlet fever and diphtheria. Since it documented my birthplace as St. Sauerbrunn, that seemed the most logical place to start. But although I searched through atlases and historical maps of Germany and all the countries Hitler's armies had invaded, there was no town or village with that name.

The closest match was the Austrian spa town of Bad Sauerbrunn, not far from the border with Hungary. I found the address of the Austrian Ministry of Foreign Affairs and wrote a lengthy letter asking if they could help me locate any record of a family called Matko anywhere in the vicinity of Bad Sauerbrunn.

I was now becoming somewhat impatient. I had not received any reply—much less any information—from the Bundesarchiv, and I was also still waiting for Georg Lilienthal to deliver the information he had supposedly found about me during his research into Lebensborn.

But what exactly was Lebensborn? And how did it connect to me? I began searching for information about this mysterious-sounding organization.

What struck me immediately was how little seemed to have been published. More than fifty years after the end of the war, the terrible history of the Third Reich and its crimes had been analyzed and picked over in meticulous detail, and yet a Google search for Lebensborn produced only a few, largely repetitive results.

Ostensibly, the Lebensborn Society—literally translated *Lebensborn* means "fount" or "source, of life"—had been founded in 1935 as a sort of welfare organization, funded by the Nazi Party, to run maternity homes across Germany; it was set up in response to what was rapidly becoming a demographic crisis for the new Reich. When Hitler came to power in the 1930s, the country's population had been falling for decades. In 1900 the statistics showed an average birthrate per thousand of 35.8; by 1932 that had dropped to 14.7. From the outset the Nazi regime set out to stop—and then reverse—the trend.

They began with innocent-sounding slogans—"Restoring the family to its rightful place" was typical—and then introduced financial incentives—marriage loans, child subsidies, and family allowances—to have a large family. A cult of motherhood was also formally established; every year on the birthday of Hitler's own mother, fertile women were awarded the Honor Cross of the German Mother. Those who produced more than four children were given a bronze medal; more than six earned silver, with gold being awarded to those who had more than eight. When this didn't produce results quickly enough, new laws were introduced to ban the advertisement and display of contraceptives and all birth-control clinics were shut down.

Abortions were criminalized as "acts of sabotage against Germany's racial future."

It was that phrase—*racial future*—that was the first clue to the reality hiding behind the seemingly innocuous Lebensborn Society. Although the ostensible aim of the homes was to allow women who might otherwise abort their pregnancy to give birth in safety and in secret—thus helping to boost Germany's population—they weren't open to everyone.

I was, of course, aware of the Nazis' obsession with race; it was the altar on which Hitler and his regime had sacrificed more than six million Jews. What I hadn't encountered was the extraordinary and convoluted web of organizations that had been established to safeguard the "purity" of the German race.

As I continued my research I could feel myself being pulled down the rabbit hole of National Socialist madness. At its heart was the sinister figure of Heinrich Himmler.

Himmler had joined the Nazi Party in August 1923, three years after its birth. He was not one of its early fanatics—his membership number was 14,303—but within six years he had taken charge of its most powerful paramilitary organization, the Schutzstaffel, more infamously known by its initials: SS.

As *Reichsführer SS*, Himmler began creating a parallel—and ultimately much more powerful—organization to control and monitor the Nazi Party. He had long been interested in the then-fashionable quasi-science of eugenics and became obsessed with the idea of a mystical past in which a Nordic race of pure-blooded warriors had conquered much of Europe. He began reorganizing the SS to be the vanguard of a reborn race of Aryan "supermen."

Under his direction applicants were vetted for their racial qualities:

he described this process as being *"like a nursery gardener trying to reproduce a good old strain which has been adulterated and debased; we started from the principles of plant selection and then proceeded quite unashamedly to weed out the men whom we did not think we could use for the build-up of the SS."*

In 1931 he created a separate department within the SS to ensure that his "plant selection" ran smoothly: Das Rasse und Siedlungs-hauptamt SS, or RuSHA. A literal translation of this phrase would be "SS Race and Settlement Main Office"; what it meant in practice was an organization dedicated to safeguarding the "racial purity" of the Schutzstaffel. One of its duties was to oversee the marriages of SS personnel; on Himmler's personal orders RuSHA issued a permit to marry only after detailed background investigations had proved that both would-be partners had an uninterrupted racial pedigree showing them to have come from pure Aryan bloodstock as far back as 1800.

As I read further, I discovered that Lebensborn had been formed and fostered under RuSHA's banner. In a circular issued on December 13, 1936, Himmler had set out both the lineage and the aims of his new organization.

> *The Lebensborn Society is under the direct personal control of the Reichsführer SS. It is an integral part of the Race and Settlement head Office and its objects are:*
>
> *1. To support racially and genetically valuable large families.*
>
> *2. To accommodate and look after racially and genetically valuable expectant mothers who, after careful investigation of their families and those of the fathers of their children by*

*RuSHA, can be expected to give birth to equally valuable children.*

*3. To look after those children.*

*4. To look after the mothers of those children.*

Even to me—a German woman, born during the war, who had lived her whole life in a country trying to come to terms with the legacy of Hitler's twisted vision—this sounded like the stuff of madness.

In German we have a very expressive word for this sort of fantastic lunacy: *unglaublich*—meaning "unbelievable." How could anyone "prove" their racial or genetic value—and what, in any event, did such a bizarre concept mean in practice?

I was not, it emerged, alone in being confused. Among the results of my Google search was a succession of references to rumors that had grown up around Lebensborn facilities. Some of these dated back to the war years and suggested that ordinary Germans had become worried by stories that these ostensible maternity homes were in fact SS stud farms: places where the cream of Himmler's brigades were introduced to suitable Aryan women in order to breed racially valuable babies for the Reich. This gossip was completely false, but the secrecy that surrounded Lebensborn had ensured that over the years, the rumors had persisted. I found that there was even an entire genre of sordid Nazi exploitation films and books that had, for several decades, spread the myth. One typical example—a movie made in 1961 by a German director and widely available on the Internet—had the English title *Ordered to Love* and a screaming subtitle, *Frauleins Forced into Nazi Breeding*!

I FELT ASHAMED and horrified. I realized that the SS stud farm stories were no more than absurd fantasies (and, as often as not, cynical attempts to sell tawdry films and novels); but if this was what the world knew—or thought it knew—about Lebensborn, was it any surprise that modern Germany was unwilling to talk openly about it? Perhaps this explained why my requests for information from the Bundesarchiv were still unanswered? Certainly I had received no response to my letter; two months had passed and I was beginning to despair.

I knew that alone I had little chance of being able to investigate Lebensborn, much less to uncover its role in my origins. I needed help, but there seemed to be a wall of silence surrounding anything to do with this corner of Nazi history.

In February 2000 my hopes dropped further. The Austrian government finally replied to my letter asking whether there was any record of a family called Matko in Bad Sauerbrunn. There wasn't, and never had been. My journey seemed to be over almost before it had started. If I hadn't come from Austria, where had I been born?

AND THEN, A few days later, a letter arrived from Georg Lilienthal in Mainz. For the first time it contained clues—solid, historical information—about Lebensborn and where it fit into my story. But Lilienthal began cautiously, hinting once again at painful secrets lying in wait for me.

*Dear Frau von Oelhafen.*

*I would first like to thank you for the trust you have placed in me with your letter because it's all about the question of your identity. Therefore, I am also glad that Ms. Fischer of the German Red Cross in her conversation with you was very careful . . . I have to apologize to you. My response to your letter took a long time. And while you were waiting for a sign from me, you might have come to doubt whether your request was the right thing to do. I can reassure you.*

*My long silence was partly due to external reasons (too little time to find the documents together and write): but on the other hand I was also aware that the answer would not be easy because I know what it could mean to you. That's why I have been writing my letter on and off since early January. That is what has led me to outline your presumptive fate so soberly and in a seemingly emotionless way. I did not want to influence your feelings with my feelings.*

*Now for your request. As you write, the fact that you have two names (Erika Matko and Ingrid von Oelhafen) has long been known. I assume that you have therefore always wondered what it's all about. Apparently your foster parents have not been completely open with the little they knew about you.*

After reading the letter, I could not have told you what exactly my feelings were: there was anxiety and apprehension but these were also shot through with excitement.

I knew, of course, that neither Hermann nor Gisela had ever told me anything approaching the truth about my origins. I had, to some extent, convinced myself that if this hadn't been the result of the tensions of postwar life, it must have been because they didn't really know my history. Reading Lilienthal's letter was the first time I had been forced to confront the possibility that my foster parents might have deliberately withheld information.

And then came the revelation I had been waiting for and half expecting. Lilienthal's research had found the name Erika Matko in some long-forgotten records of the Lebensborn program. She had been raised in one of its children's homes, a place called Sonnenwiese (literally: "Sunny Meadow") at Kohren-Sahlis. Since I was—or once had been—Erika Matko, that meant I was a Lebensborn baby. What's more, his investigations had convinced him that Hermann and Gisela had deliberately concealed this information from me.

My mind was now in turmoil. Not only did I have to face the uncomfortable revelation about my foster parents' dishonesty with me—for that is what it amounted to—but there was now solid documentary evidence linking me to this bizarre and evidently still-shameful Nazi organization; one that had been under the direct control of the SS.

And yet my overall response was exhilaration rather than shock. It all seemed incredible—but it also seemed to offer the chance for me finally to find out more about who I was and where I had come from. And in a way, the revelation also brought me a little peace. Although I did not yet understand the true nature of Lebensborn—that would come much later—I could now let go of one of the worries that I had lived with ever since I discovered that I had been fostered.

If, as my initial research indicated, Lebensborn was a political program in which the demands of the Nazi regime overrode the feelings of those it ruled, perhaps the reason my real parents had given me up was also political, not—as I had feared—the much more upsetting idea that they simply hadn't wanted to keep me. The realization brought me some comfort; but also a hint of fear. The Schutzstaffel. In some way I had been involved with an organization that, nearly sixty years later, still evoked fear and loathing. How did I begin life in the care of Himmler's fearsome creation? I mentally added the SS to the growing list of Nazi groups I would need to investigate.

Lilienthal's letter contained more surprises. Realizing that I knew little about how Lebensborn had operated, he explained how children had arrived at Sonnenweise. Some had been born in Lebensborn maternity homes then brought to Kohren-Sahlis as part of Himmler's program to increase the population of the Reich. Others, though, had apparently been kidnapped.

*Children born in this maternity home were German children born illegitimately in the Lebensborn programme for foster care or for adoption. But there were also children at Kohren-Sahlis who were trafficked from the occupied countries of Germany and who were designated for Germanization.*

I had never heard of "Germanization." What did it mean—and why would the Nazis traffic in children from the countries they had invaded? I had always been taught that Hitler and his henchmen viewed the people of many of these conquered states quite literally as subhuman. And, above all, how did this fit with what little I knew about Hermann and Gisela fostering me? Once again, Lilienthal had an answer.

*Lebensborn worked with German foster families, with the intention of later adoption after the victorious end of the war. The fall of the Third Reich prevented these plans from being realized. Most* of these foreign children returned to their home countries. However, some remained in Germany with their foster families.

There were various different reasons for this. Some of the foster parents cared for their foster families. Some of the foster parents concealed the foreign origin, even from the children themselves: for fear that the children might be removed again or that they would have a yearning to return home.

Ultimately, they were afraid to lose the love and affection of their foster children. Also, they wanted to protect the children from hostility and integration difficulties.

These were often the reasons that the children were not adopted after the war, as well as the fact that they often lacked the necessary papers.

Some of the Allies did not want to send the children back to their home countries against their will, and they remained in the German family with the authorities of their home countries in agreement because they had no biological family left.

And then Lilienthal dropped his biggest bombshell.

*Frau von Oelhafen, is it your belief that you might not be a child of German parents? I have known your name "Erika Matko," and the name of your foster parents "von Oelhafen," for many years from documents in the Bundesarchiv. I have researched Lebensborn for over twenty years and I know many of the fates of Lebensborn children.*

*Their names are mentioned in lists that were created by Lebensborn for children to be Germanized from Poland, and Yugoslavia and Czechoslovakia (in the Lebensborn management*

*they were called only Ost-Kinder) and in the records and
statements of former Lebensborn employees.*

*Although I can present to you no papers (such as a birth
certificate), giving you ultimate peace of mind, I do have
documents that seem to show that you probably originated in
Yugoslavia.*

*After you have read my letter, you may ask, What to do now?
I cannot give you the answer to this. But if you want to continue
to search for your identity, I will be happy to assist you. You can
always contact me.*

When I put down Lilienthal's letter my mind was reeling. Kidnapping, Germanization, *Ost-Kinder*; these words and notions were so completely alien to me—so far away from the assumptions I had made when I began my journey—that I didn't know what to make of them.

And now Yugoslavia. Although the Austrian authorities had been unable to find any trace of a Matko family in or near Bad Sauerbrunn, I had still believed that the search for my past would somehow take me to Austria. In a way it had been a comforting thought; the time I had spent at Innsbruck meant the country felt familiar. Nor was there any language barrier; German was the national language. Now it seemed I must start again from square one—and in a language I had never even heard spoken. Even worse, Yugoslavia itself had ceased to exist; the last of the former Iron Curtain countries had disintegrated in a bloody civil war before splintering into a series of smaller new states. Where—how—would I begin?

I decided to take Georg Lilienthal at his word; I wrote to him, asking for guidance. Throughout my journey into the past I have been very fortunate to find people who were willing to give their time and share their expertise to assist me from one stumbling step to the next. Dr. Lilienthal was the first, and probably the most important, of my guides. He told me I must write to two German ministries in Berlin— Foreign Affairs and Internal Affairs.

He helped me compose the letters, each of which explained my situation and set out my belief that I had been brought into the Lebensborn program from the former Yugoslavia: I begged both sets of officials to help me make contact with their counterparts in Eastern Europe.

My requests apparently fell on deaf ears. Both ministries sent abrupt and unhelpful replies, saying that they could not do anything for me; the only thing they could suggest was that I write to the government of Slovenia—the new nation that had emerged in the central part of Yugoslavia that Hitler's Reich had once controlled.

Around the same time I received a reply to my original inquiry at the Bundesarchiv. This, too, was unhelpful; the state archives insisted that they held nothing relevant to my history. I began to see a pattern developing: no government institution seemed interested in helping me investigate my past. Since I knew that Georg Lilienthal had already found documents relating to Erika Matko and the Sonnenwiese home in those very same archives, I was starting to understand just how reluctant German officials were to talk about Lebensborn. Over the next few months it was a reluctance I would encounter over and over again.

Georg Lilienthal pointed me toward two other, lesser-known collections of documents in which, he said, I might find information about Lebensborn. And he agreed to use his own contacts to find out who I should write to in Slovenia.

Looking back, I realize this was the pivotal point in my investigation; from here on there would be no turning back. Once I began digging into boxes of dusty papers, stored in archives across modern Germany, there was no guarantee of what skeletons I might disturb, what secrets I might unearth. But that is the benefit of hindsight; only now can I see this. At the time I don't think I paused even for a second. I was determined to find out whatever was known about me, and by extension about those who had raised me. If that meant asking questions that made people uncomfortable—well, so be it. I was eager to continue my journey and frustrated by those who were standing in my way.

I could not have known then just where my path would lead. Nor what pain I would encounter along it.

# EIGHT

# Bad Arolsen

*Adolf Hitler has led the German people to the realization that the Nordic race is the most creative, valuable race on earth. Therefore, caring for the valuable Nordic blood is their most important task.*

HEINRICH HIMMLER,
*"Racial Politics" (1943 SS publication)*

B AD AROLSEN IS a small, picture-postcard German town.

For more than 250 years it was owned and ruled by the princes of Waldeck-Pyrmont, then a sovereign principality stretching across the rich agricultural heartlands of Hesse and Lower Saxony. They constructed a large Baroque-style stately home and drew up plans to build the town around it in a mathematically perfect grid of streets. But when they ran out of money the grandiose scheme was only half completed; they compensated by landscaping the undeveloped sections with shrubbery.

Die Grosse Allee is the main street, running in one perfectly straight mile from east to west and lined by 880 German oak trees in strict military formation. Exactly halfway down is an unprepossessing piece of postwar architecture, set back from the road behind long hedge walls so as to be almost unnoticeable to the casual visitor.

Yet this building is one of the most important locations for an understanding of Hitler's Reich. This is the archive of the International Tracing Service; here, spread haphazardly over several floors and spilling out into satellite buildings, more than thirty million individual files record the fate of those who fell victim to the National Socialist criminal enterprise.

It is a cliché of modern history that the Nazis were painstaking record keepers. But the point about clichés is that they speak to a truth—however hackneyed or overfamiliar it has become. The 26,000 linear meters of original documents and 232,710 meters of microfilm housed at the ITS bear witness to this; and, according to Georg Lilienthal, somewhere in the vast piles of paperwork there was likely to be a record of how I came to be part of the Lebensborn program.

I wrote to the archive in the early spring of 2000, asking for its help in locating any document that would help me investigate my origins. In theory, this should have been a straightforward request; it was, after all, exactly what ITS was established to do. But, as I was finding, theory and practice remained a long way apart; and what separated them was often politics.

In 1943, the international section of the British Red Cross was asked by SHAEF, the Supreme Allied Headquarters in Europe, to set up a registration and tracing service for missing persons.

Even by that midstage of the war, Washington and London had begun to plan for its aftermath, and had realized that the effects of the Nazi reign of terror across the continent were certain to create a vast population of the displaced or the disappeared. The Central Tracing Bureau was established in February 1944; as the war moved eastward into each territory successively liberated from the German armies, it moved from London to Versailles, on to Frankfurt, and finally arrived at Bad Arolsen in 1946. Here its researchers set about creating an archive of Nazi documents.

The records came from every corner of the former Reich. Allied forces had rescued them from concentration and death camps, or captured them from Wehrmacht field offices and Nazi central registries. Each individual piece of paper was analyzed; from them the CTB was able to begin reconstructing the fate of tens of millions of men, women, and children who had been taken for slave labor, imprisoned, or murdered in the Holocaust.

From the outset the Allies had two sometimes conflicting aims for this unprecedented exercise. The first was to prepare reliable documentary evidence for use at the Nuremberg War Crimes Tribunal; here, for the first time in history, the surviving leaders of a country were to be put on public trial for the newly defined offenses of crimes against humanity, conspiracy to wage aggressive war, and the industrial-scale murders of Jews and Eastern Europeans (among many others).

The second, longer-term ambition was to create a mechanism to enable the survivors of the war—and especially of the Holocaust—to find their families and, if possible, eventually to reunite them. And so, the CTB began building from the captured files a central name index of every single person they could determine to have been a victim of the Nazis' reign of terror.

Whether or not the Allies realized the scale of the task when they began it, they would soon be overwhelmed by the sheer volume of cases. The central name index alone would come to house the individual fates of fifty million people. And behind each handwritten index card was a mound of paper.

As the years passed, responsibility for managing—and above all, funding—the herculean effort was passed from one organization to another. In July 1947, the newly formed United Nations International Refugee Organization took over administration of the bureau, changing its name to the International Tracing Service. Less than four years later it was handed back to the Allied High Commission for Germany—the body set up by America, Britain, and France to run their sectors of the former Reich. When the occupied status of Germany was repealed in 1954, ITS was hived off to the International Committee of the Red Cross, which promptly insisted on appointing its own manager to run all daily operations; for good measure, this appointee had to be a Swiss citizen. It was a sorry catalog of financial and administrative buck passing that ensured that the ITS was destined to be the Cinderella of the vast postwar archives mission.

The situation worsened with the implementation in 1955 of the Bonn Agreement, which formally ratified the new nation of West Germany. One clause in this document prohibited the publication of any data that could harm former victims of the Nazis or their families. However well intentioned, the instruction effectively shut the Bad Arolsen archive off from any public scrutiny; historians and journalists were not permitted to examine the fading piles of papers, and although individual victims of the tyranny were, in theory, able to ask for any relevant information, this, too, became caught up in the realpolitik of modern Europe.

At the start of 2000—just as I made my request for help—the German Parliament was under pressure to set up a fund to compensate an estimated one million survivors of the Nazis' forced and slave labor program. These were men and women who had been shipped from Eastern Europe to toil in the factories that kept Hitler's war machine running. Soon the Bundestag passed a law establishing a Remembrance, Responsibility and Future Foundation (Stiftung Erinnerung, Verantwortung und Zukunft), which would make payments to those who could prove they had been affected. The evidence they needed was primarily held at the ITS; it was almost instantly flooded with applications, and all other inquiries were either ignored or not properly processed. Among them was my letter; I received a brief, and as it would turn out completely inaccurate reply, to the effect that there was no trace of me in the files.

Seven years would pass before the ITS archives were opened to full public scrutiny, lost time that would have a terrible impact on my search for my biological family. What those very personal files—for there were several—finally revealed must wait for the proper time in my story, but if I am to explain the origins of Lebensborn I must step outside this chronology and pull back the veil of secrecy that then surrounded Bad Arolsen.

Among the millions of documents captured from the Nazi war machine were many of Heinrich Himmler's personal papers. These were sent to the ITS, where separate folders were opened, each covering the myriad organizations the *Reichsführer* had set up, as well as the bizarre and obsessive belief system that underpinned them.

The pernicious idea that one race was superior to another had begun in the last decades of the nineteenth century. By the early 1920s an entire "science" based on this had spread across Europe and the Western world. Eugenics held that since some peoples were of higher quality than others, it was naturally right to improve the overall human genetic strain by promoting higher reproduction among those people from the superior race or class and, by extension, reducing reproduction by those less well favored. However shocking this thinking seems now, at the time it was supported by the prominent English novelist H. G. Wells, as well as Marie Stopes, the founder of modern birth control, and two American presidents, Woodrow Wilson and Theodore Roosevelt.

Eugenics societies sprang up, often funded by wealthy American foundations, to promote (in the words of a 1911 Carnegie-supported research paper) "the Best Practical Means for Cutting off the Defective Germ-Plasm in the Human Population." Sterilization and euthanasia were the most popular suggested methods.

It was a belief system and a climate tailor-made for the Nazis. It played into their entirely spurious belief that Germans were the true descendants of a breed of Aryan (sometimes called Nordic) supermen whose destiny was once again to rule the world. In 1925 Hitler had promulgated this absurd concept in his autobiographical Nazi manifesto, *Mein Kampf*.

> *The products of human culture, the achievements in art, science and technology with which we are confronted today are almost exclusively the creative product of the Aryan. That very fact enables us to draw the not unfounded conclusion that he alone was the founder of higher humanity and was thus the very essence of what we mean by the term "man."*
>
> *What we must fight for is to safeguard the existence and reproduction of our race and our people, the sustenance of our children and the purity of our blood . . .*

Four years later he followed this up in a speech to a party rally.

> *If Germany were to get a million children a year and remove 700,000 to 800,000 of the weakest people, the final result might be an increase in strength.*

It was a refrain taken up by the man who would shortly become the Führer's most powerful henchman, Heinrich Himmler. When he was appointed head of the SS that same year he told his senior officers:

> *Should we succeed in establishing our Nordic race again in and around Germany . . . and from this seed bed produce a race of 200 million, then the world will belong to us. We are called, therefore, to create a basis on which the next generation can create history.*

Creating that basis began shortly after Hitler seized power in 1933. One of his first pieces of legislation was the Law for the Prevention of Hereditarily Diseased Offspring. This required doctors to register every case of hereditary illness among their female patients of childbearing age. Failure to comply was punishable by substantial fines. The opening paragraphs of the new law set out both the problem (as the Nazis saw it) and its primary cause.

*Since the National Revolution* [the quasi-legal putsch by which Hitler took to himself the power to rule by decree] *public opinion has become increasingly preoccupied with questions of demographic policy and the continuing decline in the birth rate.*

*However, it is not only the decline in population which is a cause for serious concern but equally the increasingly evident genetic composition of our people.*

*Whereas traditionally healthy families have for the most part adopted a policy of having only one or two children, countless numbers of inferiors and those suffering from hereditary conditions are reproducing without restraint, allowing their sick and disadvantaged offspring to be a burden on the community.*

The solution was—to Nazi thinking—obvious: sterilization. A system of 181 Genetic Health Courts was set up to order the enforced neutering of those deemed substandard. A measure of the immediate effect of this barbaric program was the volume and outcome of appeals: in less than a year almost 4,000 people tried to overturn the decisions of the sterilization authorities. Just 41 were successful. Five years later, by the start of World War II, at least 320,000 people had been forcibly sterilized under the legislation.

But if the draconian new law addressed the perceived problem of "inferiors" polluting or weakening the nation's bloodstock, it did nothing to define just what that should be. And so, in September 1935, a leading Nazi doctor named Gerhard Wagner announced in a speech that the government would soon introduce a *"law for the protection of German blood."* Within days this was codified into the Nuremberg Laws.

These introduced four official categories of human beings in the National Socialist state. People with four German grandparents were classified as "German or kindred blood"; those who had one or two Jewish grandparents were deemed to have come from "mixed blood" and were placed—in order of descending value—into two classes of *Mischling*; while anyone descended from three or four Jewish grandparents was simply and irredeemably a Jew.

Only those who were formally registered as being the product of "German or related blood" were now "racially acceptable" and granted the status of *Reichsbürger* (citizens of the Reich). *Mischlings* were placed in the lesser category of *Staatsangehörige* (state subjects); Jews were from that point on deprived of all citizenship rights, and marriage between Aryans and non-Aryans was outlawed.

The Nazis proceeded to formalize these race classifications. A new set of official documents—*Der Ariernachweis* (literally: the Aryan Certificates)—were introduced to prove that the holder was a true member of the Aryan race. Those able to satisfy the criteria that their racial ancestry dating back to 1800 showed that *"none of their paternal nor their maternal ancestors had Jewish or coloured blood"* were granted a *Grosser Ariernachweis* (Greater Aryan certificate). Others who could only produce seven birth or baptism certificates (covering themselves, their parents, and grandparents) as well as three marriage certificates from their parents and grandparents were provided with a *Kleiner Ariernachweis* (Lesser Aryan certificate).

Nor did the bureaucratic madness end there. Two other documents became vital for life in the Nazi state. An *Ahnenpass* was a certificate, drawn from church records, that recorded the racial characteristics of a person's ancestors. It was, quite literally, an "Ancestors' Passport." It was often supplemented by an *Ahnentafel*—a carefully drawn tabulated version of the ancestral family tree.

The Nuremberg Laws and the bizarre racial certificates that flowed from them were the first foundations of the Nazis' determination to arrive at a "Final Solution" for the Jewish population—the Holocaust. But they were also the key cornerstones of the flip side of the policy to exterminate Jews: the program to create a new master race of pure-blooded Aryans who would rule Hitler's Thousand Year Reich. The organization that was to deliver that outcome was Lebensborn; and its architect was Heinrich Himmler.

Himmler's papers contained his own explanation for establishing Lebensborn. His motive was, he claimed, benign and selfless.

*I have created the Lebensborn homes because I believe it is not right that an unfortunate girl who expects a child out of wedlock is kicked around by everybody . . . by all these paragons of virtue, of male and female gender, who feel entitled to condemn her and to mistreat her. I cannot think it right that she is being punished when the state does not provide the facility for help.*

*Every woman in these homes is addressed by her christian name. One is Frau Maria and the other Frau Elisabeth—or whatever her name is. Within the homes nobody asks whether they are married or unmarried: we simply educate them, protect them and look after these mothers.*

Even if this were true, I had to remind myself that Lebensborn homes were not open to every woman who found herself unexpectedly pregnant. Jewish women and *Mischlings* were, of course, excluded because Himmler saw them as racially worthless.

AS WAR LOOMED, the *Reichsführer's* papers also revealed a change in the purpose of the Lebensborn program. No longer was it driven simply by a desire to increase pure Aryan bloodstock within the German population. By October 1939 Himmler had looked into the near future and seen a major threat to his plans for a future master race.

> *Every war involves a tremendous loss of the best blood. Many victories won by force of arms have inflicted a shattering defeat for a nation's vitality and blood. But the sadly necessary deaths of the best men—deplorable though they are—is not the worst of this. Far more severe is the absence of the children who were never born to the living during the war, or to the dead after it.*

And so he issued a revolutionary order to the men under his command. In a proclamation marked "secret" and issued to every member of the SS and police, the *Reichsführer* instructed them to fulfill their sacred duty to the Reich by fathering its next generation, whether or not they were married to the mothers.

BERLIN, OCTOBER 28, 1939

> *Beyond the limits of bourgeois laws and conventions, which are perhaps necessary in other circumstances, it can be a noble task for German women and girls of good blood to become even outside marriage, not light-heartedly but out of a deep moral seriousness,*

*mothers of the children of soldiers going to war of whom fate alone knows whether they will return or die for Germany.*

*During the last war, many a soldier decided from a sense of responsibility to have no more children during the war so that his wife would not be left in need and distress after his death. You SS men need not have these anxieties; they are removed by the following regulations:*

*1. Special delegates, chosen by me personally, will take over in the name of the Reichsführer SS, the guardianship of all legitimate and illegitimate children of good blood whose fathers were killed in the war.*

*We will support these mothers and take over the education and material care of these children until they come of age, so that no mother and widow need suffer want.*

*2. During the war, the SS will take care of all legitimate and illegitimate children born during the war and of expectant mothers in cases of need. After the war, when the fathers return, the SS will in addition grant generous material help to well-founded applications by individuals.*

*SS-Men and you mothers of these children which Germany has hoped for show that you are ready, through your faith in the Führer and for the sake of the life of our blood and people, to regenerate life for Germany just as bravely as you know how to fight and die for Germany.*

The order did not merely authorize free sex; it demanded it. Racially pure men and women were ordered to copulate—whether or not they were married—to father children so that the nation's stock of "good blood" could be safeguarded. There was to be neither a financial penalty for producing illegitimate children nor any social stigma.

It is hard to overstate the radical nature of Himmler's decree. Although the Nazis had been in power for six years and had done much to undermine the traditional foundations of the family, Germany was still then a religiously conservative society. Sex outside marriage was taboo, and neither the public, nor the churches, were ready to abandon their social mores.

Even representatives of the Nazi Party and the Wehrmacht evidently reacted badly to the *Reichsführer*'s new population policy. Yet Himmler stood firm. Three months after his "procreation order" he issued an unyielding and unrepentant statement to his forces.

Office of the Reichsführer SS and

Chief of the German Police Berlin, 30 January 1940

SS Order for the Whole of the SS and Police

*You are aware of my order of 28 October 1939, in which I reminded you of your duty if possible to become fathers of children during the war.*

*This publication, which was conceived with a sense of decency and was received in the same sense, states and openly discusses actual problems. It has led to misconceptions and misunderstandings on the part of some people. I therefore consider it necessary for every one of you to know what doubts and misunderstandings have arisen and what there is to say about them.*

*Objection has been taken to the clear statement that illegitimate children exist, and that some unmarried and single women and girls have always become mothers of such children outside marriage and always will.*

*There is no point in discussing this; the best reply is the letter from the Führer's Deputy to an unmarried mother which I enclose together with my order of 28 October 1939.*

The Deputy Führer was Rudolph Hess. On Christmas Day 1939 the Nazi Party's daily paper, *Völkischer Beobachter*, had published an open letter to a notional unmarried mother in which Hess set out the new morality.

*The National Socialist philosophy of life having given the family the role in the State to which it is entitled, in times of special national emergency special measures can be instituted which are different from our basic principles. In wartime, which involves the death of many of our best men, every new life is of special importance to the nation. Hence, if racially unobjectionable young men going on to active service leave behind children who pass on their blood to future generations through a girl of the right age and similar healthy heredity . . . steps will be taken to preserve this valuable national wealth.*

By calling on Hess—then more established in the hierarchy of Hitler's regime—Himmler was doubtless giving himself some political cover. But his own command of the SS was absolute and his faith in its fundamental importance to the next generation unshakable.

*The worst misunderstanding* [of my original order] *concerns the paragraph which reads: "Beyond the limits of bourgeois laws and conventions . . ." According to this, as some people misunderstand it, SS men are encouraged to approach the wives of serving soldiers. However incomprehensible to us such an idea may be, we must discuss it.*

*What do those who spread or repeat such opinions think of German women? Even if, in a nation of 82 million people, some man should approach a married woman from dishonourable motives or human weakness, two parties are needed for seduction: the one who wants to seduce and the one who consents to being seduced.*

*Quite apart from our own principle that one does not approach the wife of a comrade, we think that German women are probably the best guardians of their honour. Any other opinion should be unanimously rejected by all men as an insult to German women.*

For all the *Reichsführer's* protestations of outrage, this was very far from an outright denial of the charge that he was promoting sex outside marriage. Fears about lax morals in Nazi organizations had been growing for three years; in the summer of 1937 several thousand copies of a privately printed "Open Letter to Goebbels," the party's propaganda minister, had circulated throughout the country. Signed with the pseudonym "Michael Germanicus," it pointedly referred to promiscuity throughout the National Socialist movement.

*. . . the sexual excesses in country homes and Hitler Jugend* [Hitler Youth] *camps; the bad camp morals and the Bund Deutscher Mädel* [League of German Maidens] *girls made "young mothers" . . .*

Neither the imprisonment of those caught in possession of the open letter nor Himmler's defense of his "procreation order" ever completely suppressed this deep-seated public anxiety that Lebensborn homes were being used for sexual liaisons between SS officers and suitably Aryan mates. Himmler's own statements sometimes added fuel to this quite unfounded rumor, notably an ill-chosen phrase to describe the role of the SS in the process: *"We only recommended genuinely valuable, racially pure men as Zeugungshelfer* [procreation helpers]." It was easy, with hindsight, to see where the "SS stud farms" myth of Lebensborn began.

But rumors aside, the central role of the SS in the project was beyond doubt. Himmler's statement of January 1940 set out its parental role in the Lebensborn program.

*The question has been raised as to why the wives of the SS and police are looked after in a special way and not treated the same as all the others. The answer is very simple: because the SS through their willingness to make sacrifices and through comradeship have raised the necessary funds, through voluntary contributions from leaders and men, which have been paid for years to the Lebensborn organization.*

*Following this statement all misunderstandings should have been cleared up. But it is up to you SS men, as at all times when ideological views have to be put across, to win the understanding of German men and women for this sacred issue so vital to our people and which is beyond the reach of all cheap jokes and mockery.*

If I was to understand Lebensborn—and thereby come closer to solving the mystery of who I was and where I had come from—I would have to delve into the history and nature of an organization that, more than fifty years after the end of the war, retained the power to instill fear and loathing. I would have to immerse myself in the Schutzstaffel.

# NINE

---

# The Order

---

*One basic principle must be the absolute rule for the S.S. We must be honest, decent, loyal, and comradely to members of our own blood and nobody else.*

HEINRICH HIMMLER,
*Speech to SS Officers, October 6, 1943*

WEWELSBURG CASTLE SITS on a steep bluff above the rolling hills and dense forests of North Rhine–Westphalia. It was originally built for the medieval prince-bishops who ruled the *Landkreis* of Paderborn: it was they who created its unique triangular layout of three round towers connected by massive stone walls.

In November 1933, Heinrich Himmler was touring the region; since he had taken charge of the SS he had been searching for a suitable location both to house an ideological training school and to become its spiritual headquarters. When he saw Wewelsburg, he immediately decided to commandeer it.

The *Reichsführer* had grandiose plans for his acquisition. His obsession with the mythology of Germany's past had convinced him that Westphalia was the heartland of the (entirely fictional) tradition of Aryan supermen. When he formally took control of the castle in September 1934, the *Völkischer Beobachter* informed its readers that a lavish ceremony had been held to mark the opening of an SS school dedicated to researching early Germanic history and mythology as the basis for "ideological and political training."

The Nazi daily paper did not report Himmler's real motivation: to create a redoubt that would—in his own words—be "the centre of the world after the Final Victory." And since the organization that was to deliver this triumph was the Schutzstaffel, Wewelsburg must be transformed into a fortress that served and glorified its mystical bonds of brotherhood.

The SS had begun life as a small and ragtag paramilitary force, set up to guard Hitler in the roughhouse era of the 1920s, when armed Nazis fought battles with their political opponents in the streets of southern Germany. When Himmler was promoted to head it in 1926, he was determined to transform the organization. New and deliberately sinister black uniforms replaced the previously favored provincial *Stiefelhosen*; new rules were imposed, banning smoking and instituting military drill sessions.

By the time he ascended to the formal rank of *Reichsführer SS* three years later, membership had risen from a few hundred to five thousand. And now Himmler drew up new criteria for recruitment. All applicants had to be at least 1.70 meters (five feet six inches) tall; those who wished to enter its basic ranks had to sign on for four years, rising to twelve for NCOs and twenty-five for would-be officers. Despite these strict demands, tens of thousands of men applied.

But the height requirement and years of promised service were only the beginning. From the moment he assumed control Himmler was determined to form its ranks exclusively with those of sound racial pedigree.

He drew up a grading system with which specially appointed "race experts" would assess the *Erscheinungsbild*—the physical appearance—of each applicant, before sorting them into one of five categories:

"Pure Nordic" was at the top, followed, in descending order of worth, by "Predominantly Nordic," "Light Alpine with Dinaric, or Mediterranean Additions," "Predominantly Eastern," and lastly "Mongrels of Non-European Origin." Only those placed in the top three groups were considered for membership of the new SS; the remainder were rejected out of hand.

But this was just the first hurdle. Those who passed the racial test were then subjected to a rigorous assessment of their other physical attributes. On a scale of one to nine, those who were assessed in the four top categories were deemed automatically acceptable; those whose fitness or physiques condemned them to rungs seven or worse were shown the door, while the middle-ranking levels of five and six were graciously allowed to become SS men if their zealotry for the Nazi cause outweighed their physical inadequacy.

There was, however, one criterion that was rigidly enforced. Every would-be member of whatever rank had to be able to provide documentary proof of his racial ancestry. For enlisted men, this pedigree had to stretch back to 1800; officers were required to provide evidence of their heritage from the mid-1700s. Just as ordinary citizens of the National Socialist state would soon be issued certificates proclaiming them to be greater or lesser Aryans, every member of the SS carried a *Sippenbuch*—a genealogical documentation attesting to their historic racial "health."

As I type these phrases I realize that I am struggling to find a way to express the horrific nature of this philosophy. It would be easy to reach for words like *obscene* or *grotesque*; but can they really convey the true horror? As a German woman raised in Hitler's Reich, I have always been acutely aware of where the Nazis' obsession with race ended: in global war and devastation, of course, but also in the extermination and concentration camps of Auschwitz, Treblinka, and Bergen-Belsen.

But if words cannot hope to do justice, I know—as I knew from the outset—that I must not shy away from this history. My own past was inextricably bound up with Himmler and the SS. Somewhere in their twisted ideas about race lay the truth about Lebensborn and clues that would enable me to uncover my origins.

For the *Reichsführer* was not simply intent on creating a force of racially pure men: in his mind, the SS was to be the foundation of a new generation, the begetters of a master race. This plan had first been articulated by the man Himmler appointed to head up his "Race and Settlement" organization, RuSHA: Walther Darré, a former chicken breeder who had returned to Germany from Argentina, and had written a manifesto titled "Blood and Soil"; in 1929 it was printed by the Nazi Party's own publishing house.

> *From the human reservoir of the SS we shall breed a new nobility.*
> *We shall do it in a planned fashion and according to biological*
> *laws—as the noble-blooded of earlier times did it instinctively.*

Himmler, who had also once been a chicken farmer, wholeheartedly endorsed this agricultural analogy, noting that by adopting Darré's principles it would be possible to *"attain the kind of success in the human sphere that one has had in the realm of animals and livestock."*

But the *Reichsführer* was also clear that this attempt to create an entire new generation must be kept within the SS as an organization; he had no intention of allowing members of his precious brotherhood to mate outside its strictly guarded criteria. To ensure this, in 1932 he issued a ten-point Engagement and Marriage Decree to every member of the Schutzstaffel.

> *1. The SS is an association of German men of Nordic determination selected on special criteria.*

*2. In accordance with National Socialist ideology and in the realization that the future of our Volk [people] rests upon the preservation of the race through selection and the healthy inheritance of good blood, I hereby institute the "Marriage Certificate" for all unmarried members of the SS, effective January 1, 1932.*

*3. The desired aim is to create a hereditarily healthy clan of a strictly Nordic German sort.*

*4. The marriage certificate will be awarded or denied solely on the basis of racial health and heredity.*

*5. Every SS man who intends to get married must procure for this purpose the marriage certificate of the Reichsführer SS.*

*6. SS members who marry despite having been denied marriage certificates will be stricken from the SS; they will be given the choice of withdrawing.*

*7. Working out the details of marriage petitions is the task of the "Race Office" of the SS.*

*8. The Race Office of the SS is in charge of the "Clan Book of the SS," in which the families of SS members will be entered after being awarded the marriage certificate or after acquiescing to the petition to enter into marriage.*

*9. The Reichsführer SS, the leader of the Race Office, and the specialists of this office are duty bound to secrecy on their word of honor.*

*10. The SS believes that, with this command, it has taken a step of great significance. Derision, scorn, and incomprehension do not move us; the future belongs to us!*

To assure this future, couples seeking Himmler's blessing on their nuptials had to complete an exhaustive questionnaire, detailing the color of their hair, eyes, and skin and their physical attributes, and to which, even more bizarrely, they had to affix photographs of themselves in bathing suits.

In case the purpose of all of this was unclear, the *Reichsführer* explicitly set out his reasoning in a directive to the SS about its responsibility to raise the new generation.

> *A marriage with few children is little more than an affair. I hope members of the SS, and especially its leaders, will set a good example. Four children is the minimum necessary for a good and healthy marriage.*

But Himmler also had a plan for those SS men who did not—or could not—produce offspring: the Lebensborn program. In 1936, just nine months after establishing the secretive society, he placed it under the direct control of the SS. And he made clear that childless officers would be expected to help Lebensborn place at least some of the babies born in its homes.

> *In the event of childlessness it is the duty of every SS leader to adopt racially valuable children, free of hereditary illnesses, and inculcate them in the spirit of our philosophy.*

Reading that sentence sent a chill through my bones. Himmler wanted his senior officers to adopt children. Although I was still largely in the dark about what role Lebensborn had played in my origins, I knew I had been raised in one of its homes; the knowledge that the SS had been so directly in control of the program—and therefore my infancy—did not augur well. Nor was the relationship between Lebensborn and the SS simply a matter of bureaucratic control. In the first Lebensborn prospectus, Himmler explicitly described the deep intertwining of his ostensibly benevolent society with the black-uniformed Schutzstaffel.

> *The expenses in carrying out [Lebensborn's] tasks will be met in the first instance by members' subscriptions. Every SS leader attached to head office is honour-bound to become a member. Subscriptions are graded according to the SS leader's age, income and number of children . . .*
>
> *If he is still childless at 28, a higher subscription will be due. At the age of 38 his second child should have arrived: if not, his subscription will again be increased.*
>
> *If at the appropriate ages further children have failed to appear, corresponding increases in the subscription will again become payable.*
>
> *Those who believe they can escape their obligations to the nation and the race by remaining single will pay subscriptions at a higher level that will cause them to prefer marriage to bachelorhood.*

I found it hard to reconcile the compassionate image of maternity homes with the evil reputation of the SS. How could anyone—even someone as blinkered and racially obsessed as Himmler—not have understood that the sinister Death's-Head regiments would engender fear and suspicion, not warmth and confidence? The answer, as it turned out, was that he didn't care. At the same time as he handed control of Lebensborn to the order, he wrote:

*I know there are people in Germany who feel ill when they see our black tunic. We understand this: we do not expect to be liked by too many people.*

The more I read, the more I understood that the SS was ultimately a clan; an insular and secretive one molded to fit Himmler's belief in a modern order of Teutonic knights, forever striving to find the Holy Grail of racial purity. And Wewelsburg Castle was at the center of this. Under the *Reichsführer*'s direction, the castle was reconstructed to reflect his obsession. Rooms were named after characters from mythology—one was called "Grail," another "King Arthur"—and in the crypt two special chambers were dug.

The lower one of the pair—*Der Obergruppenführersalle*—was intended for mystical rituals Himmler drew up for the twelve most senior SS leaders. Around a central eternal flame, and beneath a swastika carved into the arched roof, the *Reichsführer* planned to hold ceremonies celebrating—possibly worshiping—death.

This, then, was the organization that was supposed to be in charge of nurturing and safeguarding new life in the Lebensborn homes. More than half a century since the Third Reich ended in flames, this juxtaposition of death and life seemed the stuff of madness.

And yet Hitler, Himmler, and those leading the Nazis' self-declared mission to create the next generation of the Master Race, had declared their full faith in its "inevitable" success. Two years after the start of the war Hitler had publicly declared:

*I do not doubt for a moment that within 100 years or so from now all the German élite will be a product of the SS, for only the SS practices racial selection.*

Meanwhile, Dr. Gregor Ebner, a former GP-turned-SS officer and the man appointed by Himmler as chief medical officer for the Lebensborn program, pronounced that *"thanks to the Lebensborns in 30 years' time we shall have 600 extra regiments."*

I looked again at the prediction. A quick calculation revealed that a regiment was normally somewhere between five hundred and seven hundred men. Six hundred new regiments composed entirely of children born in Lebensborn homes? Even at the lowest estimate that would mean three hundred thousand babies.

Could there really be hundreds of thousands of people like me—children of the Lebensborn program living throughout Germany? If so, why had I never heard of these brothers and sisters in care? And even more to the point, where could I find them?

TEN

---

# Hope

---

*Beware of what you wish for in youth, because you will get it in middle life.*

JOHANN WOLFGANG VON GOETHE

F or so long I had hoped for a breakthrough.

From the moment my phone rang and the German Red Cross asked if I was interested in finding out about my family, I had thought of little else. But as the weeks and months crawled past with no response to the letters I had written to archives and government ministries, and as I immersed myself ever deeper in the obscenity of the Nazis' racial ideology, I came to accept that I had been searching for much longer. As I looked back, my whole life seemed to have been overshadowed by secrecy. No matter how hard I worked, no matter how much I gave of myself to the poor, damaged children who came to my practice, nothing could free me from the unhappiness of not knowing who I was. And so I had longed and hoped and dreamed.

The phone call from the Red Cross had broken the spell. No longer was I half asleep, seeing snatches of my past only in dreams; the promise of solid, reliable information had woken me. And I yearned all the harder for it.

"Be careful what you wish for," warned Germany's most famous poet, writer, and statesman. Perhaps I should have listened to old Goethe.

The letter arrived in October 2000. It was from a Jože Goličnik, the director of an archive in Maribor, Slovenia's second city and the capital of the Lower Styria region. I had heard that an old repository of parish documents was held there and, having heard nothing back from the government of Slovenia, had decided to try my luck with the church. I'd written purely on chance, with little faith that it would yield anything useful. I was wrong: Mr. Goličnik said he had found a record of my family.

> *The father of Erika Matko is Johann Matko from Zagorje ob Savi. Her mother came from Croatia. Mr Johann Matko lived in Sauerbrunn and was a glass maker.*

Sauerbrunn. It existed. Not in Austria but in Slovenia—or more accurately in the old Yugoslavia. I was so happy that quite spontaneously (and in a way most unlike me) I quite literally burst into song, singing my heart out with joy and relief and excitement. I realized, of course, that I still had to locate this Sauerbrunn and that it was not likely to be called that now; the fall of communism had been slower in Yugoslavia than elsewhere across the eastern bloc, but when it happened it brought civil war in its wake.

When the smoke of the bloody years in which Serbs fought Croats, Bosnians, Montenegrins, and all the rest of the nationalities Tito had welded into a unified republic in the 1940s had cleared, new nations rose from the ashes; many changed the names of their towns and cities.

But Mr. Goličnik's letter had contained a clue: Johann Matko had been a glassmaker. If I could find a region that had contained major glass factories, I stood a chance of tracking down Sauerbrunn and finding its new name. Better still, attached to the letter was a copy of the parish records themselves, including the Matkos' birth dates. Johann had been born on December 12 1904; his wife—Helena Haloschan—was eleven years younger, having been born in St. Peter, Croatia, on August 8, 1915.

I wrote again to the government of Slovenia, updating my original request with the information from Maribor. But I decided my best bet was to contact the German Red Cross. They had, after all, been the instigator of my investigation, and I felt sure that if anyone could help me track down the Matkos and Sauerbrunn, it would be their staff. I sent off the latest in my growing volume of letters. And then I began to research glassmaking in the former Yugoslavia.

Glass had been a regional specialty of Lower Styria for more than three centuries. From the 1700s onward factories had sprung up producing highly prized and beautifully crafted lead crystal.

The center of this tradition was the town of Rogaška Slatina: its previous name was Sauerbrunn. I had tracked down the birthplace of Erika Matko. I had found my home.

How do I describe my feelings at that moment? How can mere words express the elation of finally—after so many years—knowing where I had come from and the names of my biological parents? I felt that I could almost reach out and touch them—and that surely soon I would be able to?

Be careful, said Goethe, and he was right.

My optimism lasted only a few weeks before reality intruded. The Red Cross wrote back saying it had no information about anyone called Matko from Yugoslavia in its records of those whom the Nazis had captured or killed. Worse, it advised that it was unable to carry out any research in the archives of former Yugoslavian countries and warned that if I chose to do my own research, there was a very high probability I would discover that Erika Matko's parents were dead and that they had not died of natural causes. The message was clear: whatever records of their existence might once have existed, my parents were likely to have been killed by the Nazis after Hitler's armies invaded Yugoslavia, and, most likely, any trace of them would have disappeared at that point.

But the note from the Red Cross was not the worst of it. In February 2001 I received the letter that dashed all my hopes of ever finding my family.

The Slovenian government had been neither quick nor helpful in the months since I had first written asking for information. Now, when it did finally send a substantive response, the letter hit me like a blow to the stomach.

> *We wish to inform you that, according to the local administration of Rogaška Slatina they have discovered* [records of] *an Erika Matko, born on November 11, 1941. But this woman is still living inside Slovenia: therefore the assumption that Ingrid von Oelhafen was born as Erika Matko is wrong.*

How many blows can a person withstand? How many times can a body take punches and remain standing? More even than the body, how many disappointments, how much hurt, can the mind absorb before it cracks and splinters under the onslaught? Even as I type these words I know the truth. I realize that the generation from which my parents—whoever they were—came had known more physical suffering than I would ever experience. But the cruelest trick, the most damaging pain of all, is the torment of being offered hope and the tentative reaching out to grasp it—and then seeing it snatched away from your grasp.

I sat at the table in my flat. I held the letter in my hand. And the dreams and hopes I had believed in dissolved in front of me. Please believe me; this was not self-pity. This was not the easy melancholy with which we sometimes cosset ourselves; for the first time I had to face up to the fact that I was nothing, no one. I had known for decades that I was not truly Ingrid von Oelhafen. I had salved that wound with the belief—no, the knowledge, derived from the few scraps of paper that had traveled with me through the years—that I was once Erika Matko. Now I was neither Ingrid nor Erika. I was, truly, no one.

When the shock wore off I took time to reflect on the toll this quest for my identity was taking. I made myself look at how the ups and downs of my investigation were affecting me and realized that I had spent a whole year riding what amounted to an emotional roller coaster, soaring up high one minute, plunging down the next. And I asked myself whether it was really necessary—or even worth it? After all, I had made a life—a successful and generally happy life—as Ingrid von Oelhafen; and I had official German papers that said that I was Ingrid. Really, what did it matter that I might—or might not—have once been called Erika Matko? Would it truly make me any happier to solve the mystery of this Erika, her biological parents, and the country where she started life?

I DECIDED THAT the answer was no. I bundled all my letters, all my research notes, into a file and put it away in a drawer. I resolved to forget about them, at least for the time being. Even when—finally—

the archivists at Bad Arolsen wrote to me with the news that they had, after all, found some documents relating to Erika Matko and Lebensborn, I simply filed the letter away with all the other documents.

Months flew by, then a full year. I buried myself in work and distracted my mind by immersing myself in studying music. I had been learning to play the flute. Now I practiced harder, losing myself in the notes and the melodies of classical composers.

By the time the envelope dropped onto my doormat, a year and a half had passed since I had put away my folder marked "Erika Matko." Perhaps if the letter had been from anyone else it might have joined all the others. But this note was from Georg Lilienthal; and it contained an invitation. For the first time ever, a group of Lebensborn children was to meet. Would I like to come?

Would I? Honestly, I was not sure. Could I face returning to my journey—one that had proved to be full of dead ends, false trails, and seemingly insurmountable obstructions? Did I really want to risk opening up old wounds all over again? And even if the answer to those questions was yes, what did I actually have to contribute to the meeting?

I took out my abandoned file of paper, with its obscure Nazi documents and contradictory modern correspondence. What could I really tell anyone? I agonized, turning the whole business over in my mind again and again.

In the end I realized that I had no choice. I could no longer shut away the mystery in a drawer and pretend it didn't exist. The questions about where and who I came from had been part of my life ever since the day Frau Harte, my foster father's housekeeper, had told me I was not Hermann and Gisela's real daughter. They had been at the back of my mind, pressing down on my emotions—and perhaps shaping my actions—for more than fifty years. Hiding from them simply didn't work. I would have to go to the meeting.

And so, in October 2002 I packed up my car and began the long drive south. It was 260 kilometers from my home in Osnabrück to the town where the meeting was being held. I was leaving my refuge and place of safety and setting out on a new journey into what seemed certain to be a dangerous and painful past. I was sixty-one years old. It was time to learn about my childhood.

# ELEVEN

## Traces

*We aren't perfect. We've got all the same illnesses and disabilities as other people.*

RUTHILD GORGASS, LEBENSBORN CHILD

H ADAMAR IS A small town between Cologne and Frankfurt. It sits on the southern edge of the Westerwald, the long, low mountain range running down the eastern bank of the river Rhine.

It is known today for its highly regarded institutes devoted to forensic and social psychiatry, and for a stark obelisk commemorating the victims of the Nazis' "Aktion T-4" euthanasia program. Research by Georg Lilienthal and other historians had discovered that between 1941 and 1945 thousands of handicapped or otherwise "undesirable" men, women, and children were brought to Hadamar to be sterilized or put to death.

These actions were in keeping with the ideas about racial purity and eugenics developed by German researchers. Although Aktion T-4 officially ended in 1941, the program actually lasted until the German surrender in 1945. In total nearly fifteen thousand German citizens were sent to the hospital and had died there: most were murdered in a gas chamber. This was the place where I was to meet other Lebensborn children.

They were not, of course, children any longer. Like me, the twenty men and women sitting around the room that morning in October were in their sixties and close to retirement. As I took my seat I was very nervous. One by one we introduced ourselves; when it came to my turn I made myself speak the single sentence I had rehearsed. *"My name is Ingrid von Oelhafen. I don't know anything."* And then I burst into tears.

My companions were kind and caring. Each was much further into their personal investigations than I, and because they, too, had been through the same emotions, they sympathized with my anxiety. Gradually, as they told their stories, I began to understand the callous brutality of the Lebensborn program; and though each new revelation was a terrible shock, I also found that learning the truth somehow put me at my ease.

Ruthild Gorgass had been one of the first Lebensborn children to reach out and find others who had been born or brought up in the program. She was around my age, tall with blue eyes and a brush of short blond hair. Like me, she was a physiotherapist, and she, too, possessed a diary kept by her mother that had helped her understand the story of her birth. I liked her immediately and felt comforted by her presence.

Her story was also a good introduction to Lebensborn. Her father was forty-nine when Ruthild was born. He had been a lieutenant in the German Army during the First World War. In 1916 he was badly injured at the battle of Verdun, his back and chest a mass of shrapnel splinters.

In the 1930s he had become a committed Nazi, and by the start of World War II he was a big shot in the vital chemical industry. He was also married with a teenage son. Despite this, at some point he met and began an affair with Ruthild's mother. She was a clerk in the

Leipzig Chamber of Commerce, eighteen years younger than he; just before Christmas 1941 she found that she was pregnant. Her position fit exactly Himmler's original aim for Lebensborn: both her parents were dead, she was unmarried, carrying an illegitimate child, and therefore at risk of the opprobrium of her family and prejudice from her community. Above all, her father was a card-carrying Nazi and both he and her mother were able to demonstrate their racial purity going back the required number of generations. In the summer of 1942 they jointly made the 170-kilometer journey from Leipzig to Wernigerode, a small town deep in the spectacular Harz Mountains of Saxony. Here, in the heartland of old Germany, Himmler had established a Lebensborn maternity unit. And here, in August 1942, Ruthild was born.

HEIM HARZ, I learned, was one of twenty-five Lebensborn homes established across Germany and in the countries its armies overran. There were nine homes in Germany itself, two in Austria, eleven in Norway, and one each in Belgium, Luxembourg, and France. Often they occupied buildings stolen from Hitler's political enemies or wealthy Jewish families; the organization's central headquarters in Munich had belonged to the writer and exiled anti-Nazi activist Thomas Mann.

Some of the premises were also furnished with property confiscated from people who had been sent to the death camps, and they were filled with state-of-the-art medical equipment to ensure that Himmler's precious pure-blood babies were delivered safely into the world.

And they were. In 1939 Dr. Gregor Ebner, Lebensborn's chief medical officer, sent a report to Himmler detailing the success of the program.

More than 1,300 pregnant women had applied to give birth in the homes. Racial and hereditary health examinations had reduced this number by half, so that a total of 653 mothers-to-be were admitted. The neonatal mortality rate for Germany as a whole at the time was 6 percent; in the comfort of Lebensborn this figure was cut in half.

> *The births are very easy, without many complications. This is attributable to the racial selection and the quality of the women we get.*

All of this success came at a price. Ebner reported that the cost per mother was a very substantial four hundred Reichsmarks. But, he noted, *"that isn't much of a sacrifice if you can save a thousand children of good blood."*

Blood was all-important. Lebensborn was charged with providing and ensuring the next generation—a racially selected future master race to rule over the global empire of Hitler's Thousand Year Reich. There was even a slogan that encapsulated the duty of the women who gave birth in the homes: *"Schenkt dem Führer ein Kind"*—give a child to the Führer.

But while the physical health of the Lebensborn mothers was uppermost in Himmler's mind, he was also determined to monitor and guide their political well-being. To ensure that they left the homes even more zealous Nazis than when they arrived, women were required to attend sessions of ideological "education" every week of their stay. During these classes they were shown propaganda films, made to read chapters from *Mein Kampf,* listen to radio lectures, and join in communal singing of party anthems.

The staff, too, was both carefully monitored and instructed to complete detailed questionnaires about each of the mothers under their care.

These *RF Fragebogen* (the initials stood for *Reichsführer*) recorded every aspect of the women's personalities—from their behavior in the home, their bravery (or otherwise) during birth, and their commitment to the National Socialist cause; every record was sent to Berlin, marked for the personal attention of the *Reichsführer SS*.

Nor was this just a bureaucratic nicety. Even in the midst of the war—at a time when he was overseeing the wholesale murder in the death camps and the entire apparatus of the Nazi terror throughout Europe—Himmler applied himself devotedly to these questionnaires, deciding, on a case-by-case basis, whether a woman would be allowed to give birth to a second child in Lebensborn at any point in the future.

In fact, he supervised every aspect of life in the homes, from the seemingly trivial to the bizarrely absurd. On one occasion he instructed his personal aide, SS-Stamdartenführer Rudolph Brandt, to write to the head of Lebensborn demanding that a record be kept of nose shapes.

*The Reichsführer SS wants a special card index to be kept of all mothers and parents having a Greek nose or the rudiments of one. As an example of the type required, you should refer to the mother in Questionnaire L6008, Frau I.A.*

Himmler's hands-on control extended to the diet provided for the mothers of his new generation of superbabies. He issued a stream of memos, instructing cooks on the correct way to steam vegetables and demanding that the homes' supervisors make the women eat porridge—apparently because he had identified this as a vital factor in forming the racially admirable characteristics of the English aristocracy. For good measure he also insisted on regular doses of cod-liver oil—much to the evident disgust of the recipients. He also regularly visited the homes, checking up on the progress of the women and the babies. So complete was his involvement that babies born on Himmler's birthday were formally registered as his godchildren and received a special memento—a silver cup, engraved with his name as well as that of the baby.

I found these bizarre details of life in Lebensborn bewildering. How did the second most powerful man in the Reich find the time to control day-to-day life in the twenty-five individual homes? And why?

But such oddities were quickly pushed into the background. The stories told by the Lebensborn children that day in Hadamar revealed a much darker, more sinister side to the homes. And its heart was the Schutzstaffel.

Ruthild told me that she and other children underwent a quasi-religious naming ceremony in which they were dedicated to Hitler and the brotherhood of the SS.

This *Namensgebung* ritual was a distorted version of the traditional Christian baptism, with an altar draped in a swastika flag and with a bust or a photo of the Führer in pride of place. In front of a congregation made up of Lebensborn staff and black-uniformed SS officers, mothers like Ruthild's promised that their children would be raised as good National Socialists; they then handed over their babies to an SS man who intoned a "blessing." There appeared to be different versions of this liturgy in different homes, but the essence of each was the same.

> *We believe in the god of all things*
> *And in the mission of our German blood*
> *Which grows ever young from German soil.*
> *We believe in the race, carrier of the blood,*
> *And in the Führer, chosen for us by God.*

Then an SS dagger was held over the baby and the senior officer intoned a formal welcome to the brotherhood of the SS.

*We take you into our community as a limb of our body. You shall grow up in our protection and bring honour to your name, pride to your brotherhood and inextinguishable glory to your race.*

I was shaken by these accounts. How could a mother hand over her precious baby to the care—if that's what it was—of an organization like the SS? What sort of parent could do something so horrific? And I began to wonder if this had happened to me. As I had told the gathering right at the start, the only thing I knew about my origins was that I had been a baby in the Lebensborn home at Kohren-Sahlis. Had I, too, been dedicated to the service of the Nazis?

There were more terrible revelations to come. I knew, of course, that Himmler had created Lebensborn to raise a pure-blooded Aryan generation. But I had not realized just how far his organization would go to ensure that this *Herrenrasse*—this master race—was free of any physical defect.

They called them *Kinderfachabteilung*. Literally translated this means "children's ward." It sounds like such an innocent phrase; but it wasn't. As part of the Aktion-T-4 euthanasia program, babies born in the Lebensborn homes with developmental delay, disease, or mental disabilities were killed.

Jürgen Weise was born in the Lebensborn home at Bad Polzin on June 5, 1941. The head of Lebensborn—a committed Nazi named Max Sollman—ordered that Jürgen be taken to a *Kinderfachabteilung* in Brandenburg, near Berlin. There he was given tranquilizers and deliberately left untended and unfed. On February 6, 1942, the little boy died; he was eight months old.

Jürgen Weise was not the only handicapped baby to be murdered in the name of racial purity and strength. In 2002, when we met, research into this was at an early stage—hampered by the reluctance of official archives to allow access to Nazi-era documents; but the Brandenburg *Kinderfachabteilung* had been exposed several years before, and there was convincing evidence that 147 children were murdered there—including an unknown number sent there by Lebensborn.

I found it hard to absorb—let alone comprehend—this story. I had dedicated my life to handicapped children. I had seen the joy that my efforts brought to them and to their parents. I had felt the love that comes from helping little boys like Jürgen overcome their disability. What sort of heartless bureaucrat could so easily extinguish such precious life? I added Max Sollman to the list of names I wanted to research.

Perhaps today my reaction sounds strange and a little foolish. We know, of course, that the Nazis ruthlessly and quite openly murdered millions of Jews in camps like Auschwitz and Bergen-Belsen. Why would the deaths of a few babies, born in secret and hidden from public view, matter to men such as Himmler and Hitler? But according to their own twisted ideology, these children were special: they were only born in Lebensborn because their parents had been examined, assessed, and ultimately proven to be suitable bloodstock for the master race. I simply could not process the information.

And then I looked around me at the men and women who had been part of the Lebensborn program. I looked over every body, searched each face for any evidence that these survivors—for that is what they must be—of Himmler's experiment were truly superhuman beings. Were they taller, stronger, healthier than anyone else?

Ruthild answered my unspoken question. She took off her glasses,

Ingrid, age nearly three, with Dietmar, the boy she
believed to be her brother.
*Courtesy of Ingrid Matko-von-Oelhafen*

Hermann and Gisela von Oelhafen
with Ingrid and Dietmar, Bandekow,
summer 1944.
*Courtesy of Ingrid Matko-von-Oelhafen*

Ingrid, age eleven, at Bad Salzuflen
*Courtesy of Ingrid Matko-von-Oelhafen*

The Lebensborn home, Sonnenwiese, in 1942, from a wartime postcard.

Ingrid, age twenty-one,
with Hubertus, her foster
mother's son.

*Courtesy of Ingrid Matko-von-Oelhafen*

The Lebensborn logo, from the Lebensborn Society brochure, circa 1939.

The Nuremberg Laws' Racial Identification Chart, 1935, showing the racial classifications between Germans, *Mischelinge* ("crossbreeds"), and Jews. Only those with four German grandparents were considered to be of German blood.

*Markus Moors, Wewlesburg Castle Museum*

The four most senior Lebensborn officials, photographed before their trial at Nuremburg in 1947.

SOLLMANN, Max

TESCH, Guenther

VIERMETZ, INGE

EBNER, Gregor

Heinrich Himmler inspects SS troops.

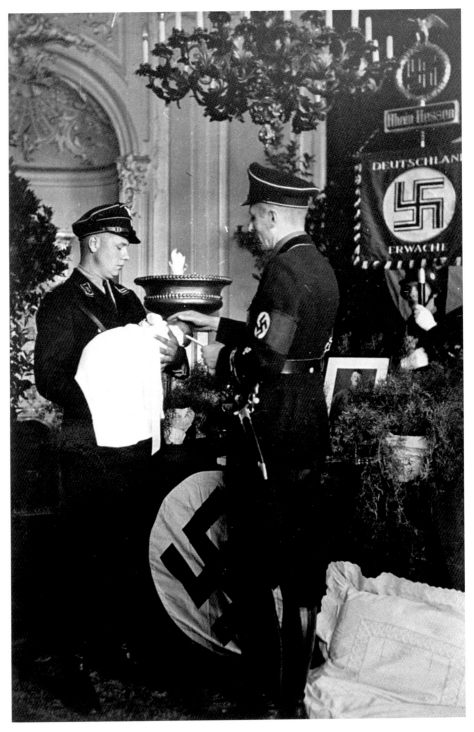

A Lebensborn baby is handed over to the care of the SS during the
*Namensgebung* "baptism" ritual inside a Lebensborn home.

*Bundesarchiv, Germany*

An SS officer intones the *Namensgebung* liturgy, with the baby lying in front of an altar dedicated to Adolf Hitler.

*Bundesarchiv, Germany*

A boy's head is measured using calipers during a racial examination, 1937.

*bpk/Fritz Carl*

The SS flag flies outside a Lebensborn home.

*Bundesarchiv, Germany*

The schoolyard, Celje, formerly Yugoslavia, August 1942. Mothers plead in vain with German soldiers as their children are taken away for racial examination. Ingrid and her parents were among them.

*Josip Pelikan / Museum of Recent History, Celje*

Stari Pisker prison, Celje, formerly Yugolsavia, summer 1942. Partisans are lined up against a wall prior to being shot.

*Museum of Recent History, Celje*

Stari Pisker prison, Celje, formerly Yugolsavia, summer 1942. The partisans' bodies lie where they fell.

*Museum of Recent History, Celje*

Inside the school, Celje, formerly Yugoslavia, August 1942.
The children were held in makeshift enclosures, packed with straw,
as they waited for their racial examinations.

*Josip Pelikan / Museum of Recent History, Celje*

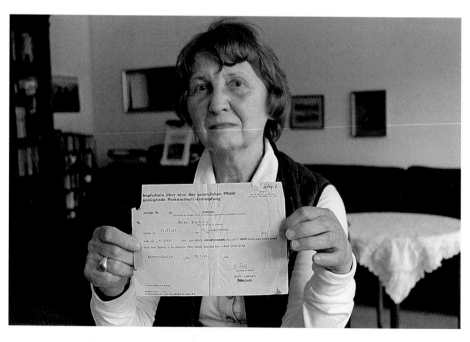

Ingrid Matko-von-Oelhafen today, with the first official document
of her existence, a vaccination certificate issued by Lebensborn.

*Courtesy of Tim Tate*

rubbed her eyes, and said: "We aren't perfect. We've got all the same illnesses and disabilities as other people."

What, then, was it all for? Himmler's great dream was a generation of super Aryans who would be so strong, so flawless that they would grow up to become the natural aristocracy of the National Socialist state and the lesser nations it ruled. Yet it seemed to have produced nothing more striking than the group of perfectly ordinary men and women seated around me.

There were, though, two very striking characteristics of most of these Lebensborn children: deep emotional hurt and a palpable sense of shame. The former stemmed from a problem with which I could easily sympathize. Because they had begun life in such a clandestine program, each had grown up with the pain of not being able to discover the truth about his or her birth.

This secrecy was both deliberate and carefully managed from the outset. Doctors and staff in the Lebensborn homes were required to swear an oath of silence that committed them to respecting *"the honour of pregnant women, whether they conceived before or after marriage,"* and in June 1939, Himmler had issued an order to protect the identity of illegitimate children born in Lebensborn homes.

*Following an agreement between the Reich Minister of the Interior and the L organization, it is possible to maintain secrecy about the origin of illegitimate children born in Lebensborn homes for an unlimited period. The Reich office will provide a certificate confirming the child's Aryan descent. This certificate can be produced by a child born in a Lebensborn home when they start school, for the Hitler Youth and for institutions of higher education, without the slightest difficulty arising.*

This determination to throw a cloak of confidentiality over all aspects of the Lebensborn children extended to the records kept of their deliveries. Himmler's organization set up a special registry office for recording the births; this was kept separate from any other office of the Reich and operated in total secrecy. Mothers' names might be shown in the files, but the identity of the father was generally deliberately omitted.

And many of these deliberately redacted records had themselves disappeared; in the final days of the war, with Allied forces closing in on the homes, Lebensborn staff destroyed much of the organization's paperwork. As a result, most of the children born in Lebensborn's homes grew up not knowing who their father was—and, unless their mothers broke the bonds of secrecy, completely unable to find out.

In particular, this affected the children who had been handed over to foster parents. But even those who, like Ruthild, were kept by their biological mothers often found it impossible to prize out the information. Many mothers were very vague about their time in Lebensborn homes; others refused point-blank to discuss it.

I knew how that felt. Although I didn't yet understand how I fit in to the story of Lebensborn, I was very familiar with walls of parental secrecy; as Georg Lilienthal had warned me, Gisela undoubtedly withheld much of what she knew throughout my life.

Why did other mothers do this, too? The reason was the second characteristic evident in many of the Lebensborn children sitting beside me in Hadamar. Shame is a powerful emotion and the political climate in postwar Germany was hardly conducive to honesty about involvement with an organization as reviled and feared as the SS.

One of the men in our little group talked openly about the guilt and the shame that had blighted his life. And his story opened my eyes to another aspect of the Lebensborn program. Hannes Dollinger had grown up in Bavaria, where the couple he thought of as his parents owned an inn. But after he started school, he heard rumors that he was a foundling. He asked his parents whether this was true, but they refused to answer, and when he persevered they punished him and forbade him from ever mentioning the subject again.

It was not until he was fifty that he learned the truth. Just as Frau Harte had once broken the news to me that Hermann and Gisela were not my real parents, a former employee of Hannes's family told him on her deathbed that he had been adopted. That alone was a shock, but the story of how he came to Bavaria was far worse.

Norway was the northernmost country occupied by Hitler's army. The Wehrmacht invaded in April 1940, and from then until the end of the war the country was run by a collaborationist government that enthusiastically did the Nazis' bidding. Himmler had for many years viewed the largely blond and blue-eyed local population as de facto Aryans. He and his officials actively encouraged liaisons between SS or Wehrmacht troops and Norwegian women, and established a network of Lebensborn homes in which the resulting babies were born, then shipped back to the Reich and handed over to suitable couples either for adoption or fostering.

The legacy of this collaboration was long and bitter. Unlike the desperate bonfires built by Lebensborn staff across Germany, in Norway the SS never managed to destroy its files. As a result, after the war thousands of Lebensborn babies and their mothers were identified and faced the fury of their countrymen. Women and their children were harassed by schoolmates or neighbors. Police arrested between three thousand and five thousand women who had slept with Germans and marched them off to internment camps. The head of Norway's largest mental hospital publicly stated that women who had mated with Germans were "mental defectives" and pronounced that 80 percent of their children were retarded.

Hannes discovered that he was one of these children. He began researching his origins and learned that his real name was Otto Ackermann and that he was born in September 1942 in a Lebensborn home near Oslo. From there he had been sent like a parcel across Germany, firstly to a Lebensborn home in Klosterheide, near Berlin, then on to Kohren-Sahlis, the home in which I had been raised.

Eventually, after being transported to the Lebensborn home in what was now Poland, he was handed over to his adoptive parents in Bavaria. It took many years for him to trace this long and complicated route. Finally he managed to obtain the name of his natural mother, but by the time he discovered this, she had died. His father—a Wehrmacht soldier—had been killed in the last months of the war. His adoptive parents had also passed away.

Hannes was, in many ways, typical of our generation of Germans—ironically, since of course he wasn't actually German. He was then a local government official and a stickler for doing things by the book. He informed the federal government that his real name was Otto Ackermann and that he was originally Norwegian, and asked to change his identity documents to make them accurate. For his trouble, the government declared him stateless—and by law stateless people were forbidden from employment in any public office. It took two long and difficult years before he was offered German citizenship, but even then, to get it he had to give up his original name.

It was heartbreaking to listen to Hannes's story. So much of it mirrored my own life—the home at Kohren-Sahlis, the problem of being declared stateless—but his experiences seemed to have been much worse. I began to feel almost lucky, and perhaps grateful, that I knew so little about where I had come from.

But at the same time I knew that this question was still very much hanging over me. I had learned a great deal about the Lebensborn program and about life in its homes. But I still did not know how I fit into this history. The documents I had found in Gisela's room showed that I had been fostered as part of something called Germanization. Neither Ruthild's story nor Hannes's contained anything to shed light on this mysterious word.

And then another member of the group stood up to speak. And for the first time I began to grasp the worst horror of Himmler's terrible experiment—and how I had come to be a part of it.

Folker Heinecke was six months older than me. He was a big man, well dressed, who had made his fortune as a shipping broker in Hamburg and in London. But though he was financially well off, for much of his life he had been deeply troubled by the knowledge that he had been raised in a Lebensborn home, and that in 1943 the organization had arranged his adoption.

> *My first memory is of being in a room with thirty other children. I remember these people coming in, while we were lined up like pet dogs to be chosen for a new home. The people were to be my parents. They went away and came back a day later. My "mother" apparently wanted a girl, but my "father" wanted a boy who would be able to take on his family business in the future. I laid my head on his knee and that did it for him—I was to be their son.*

Folker's new family was well off and well connected. Adalbert and Minna Heinecke were fanatical Nazis, and owned a successful Hamburg shipping company. Adalbert was also deaf and, under Lebensborn's strict rules, should not have been allowed to foster—let alone adopt—one of its precious children.

But Adalbert was also a personal friend of Heinrich Himmler; both the *Reichsführer* and Martin Bormann, Hitler's personal secretary and one of the most powerful men in the Nazi regime, came for visits to the family's home.

Like many other Germans, the Heineckes kept a flock of hens. Since the *Reichsführer* had once been a chicken farmer and was a firm believer in applying the principles of poultry breeding to the human species, it seemed only natural that he and Adalbert talked as they studied the family's birds. When they had finished, Himmler agreed to rubber-stamp Folker's adoption.

Folker remembered that his childhood had been happy. Even at the height of the Allied assault on Germany, when he watched RAF bombers weave through the flak and searchlights to launch raids into enemy territory, his chief memory was of finding the war exciting. Thanks to the family's wealth, he never went hungry, and it was not until after the war that he realized he had been adopted.

*One of the local kids I was playing with said: "You know you're a bastard, don't you, they're not your real mum and dad." But back then I didn't really know what that meant.*

The Heinecke family never talked to Folker about where he had come from or how he came to be adopted. When his father retired Folker took over the shipping business and enjoyed a successful career.

But in 1975 both his parents died; while going through his father's paperwork he found a series of official documents he had never seen before. These recorded that he had been born at Oderberg in Upper Silesia; this area had been annexed into Hitler's Reich, but after the war it had been transferred back into the territories of the new republic of Poland. The papers also indicated (falsely, as it turned out) that both of his biological parents had died—hence the need for his adoption.

The discovery led Folker to investigate his origins. He approached the German Red Cross, the British Army of Occupation, the American authorities, and more than thirty other agencies and church offices. Slowly he began piecing together the confusing jigsaw puzzle of his past. But Poland was then still locked away behind the Iron Curtain; it was difficult—even for a man of his wealth—to gain access to its archives. It would not be until the fall of communism and the restructuring of Eastern Europe after 1989 that he finally unearthed the truth.

By 1941, HIMMLER's great hope that the Lebensborn program would produce tens of thousands of racially pure babies was fading fast. In part this was due to the rigorous selection criteria that caused more than half of the pregnant women who applied to give birth in the network of homes to be rejected.

Nor had the SS lived up to its leaders' expectations; the SS members failed to meet the minimum requirement of fathering at least four children, and the birth rate stayed stubbornly around 1.5. The six hundred new battalions of Lebensborn babies predicted by its chief medical officer, Gregor Ebner, were a very long way off—if they were achievable at all.

Nonetheless the Nazi leaders knew that these future warriors would be needed if the Thousand Year Reich was to survive. Hitler's vision had always been for a total and global war, followed by permanent occupation of conquered lands. But by 1941 the war was claiming thousands of German lives a week. Himmler's plan for a new generation of pure Aryan babies in Lebensborn homes could not hope to fill the gap. And so he decided on a new strategy: he issued secret instructions to his troops and officials to kidnap "racially valuable" children from the countries they overran.

I FOUND IT hard to take in what Folker was saying. How could anyone—even someone as vicious and heartless as the *Reichs-führer SS*—have ordered the wholesale stealing of children? But it was true; there was even a recording of Himmler giving a private speech to SS officers during which he justified the policy.

> *What good blood there is of our kind in these peoples, we will take in, we will steal the children if necessary and bring them up here with us.*

The name given to this plan was Germanization. It was the word on my documents that I had never understood. Now I began to understand what it meant in practice.

Folker's tragedy was that at the age of two he looked German: he had blond hair, blue eyes, and appeared for all the world like a pure-blooded Aryan boy. Because of this, he was snatched from his parents by SS officers and taken to a medical institute for a full racial assessment.

> *I was measured everywhere—head size, body size—and doctors checked to be sure that I had no "Jewish Aspects." When I passed those tests the Nazis declared I was capable of being Germanized and shipped me off to a Lebensborn home in the Fatherland.*

After a brief stay at the home in Bad Polzin, he was sent on to the same place shown on my documents: Kohren-Sahlis. There were no completely reliable dates for his arrival there, but from what he had discovered, it appeared that we must have been in the home at the same time. The thought excited me and I tried hard to unearth a memory from the back of my mind; but I could recall nothing about the place. It was immensely frustrating to be so tantalizingly close to someone with whom I might have shared my earliest years and yet to be unable to dredge up any fragmentary image from my brain.

There were other similarities in our stories. Folker's documents indicated that he had been picked up by the Heinecke family from Kohren-Sahlis. That was, I knew, where Hermann and Gisela had come to collect me. Had I been lined up for inspection, one of the "pet dogs"—as Folker described it—to be examined by my prospective foster-parents?

Folker's investigations had also revealed that Lebensborn gave completely new identities to the kidnapped foreign babies shipped to its homes, and then deliberately issued false documents proclaiming them to be either German orphans or ethnically Aryan children of the German diaspora: *Volksdeutsche*. Once again I recognized that word; it was how Lebensborn had described me on the papers I found when clearing out Gisela's room.

The clues were beginning to add up. According to my documents, I had been born Erika Matko, a *Volksdeutsches mädchen*. I had been brought from Sauerbrunn (wherever that was) and transported to the Lebensborn home at Kohren-Sahlis for Germanization, before being handed to the von Oelhafens to be brought up as a "real" German girl. I was, in fact, part of the scheme to *Schenkt dem Führer ein Kind*. I was one of Hitler's children.

It was horrific to know that I had been part of something so cold, so calculating; and yet for the first time in years I felt that I was finally getting close to solving the mystery of who I really was.

The biggest remaining question was whether I was (or had once been) Erika Matko: the Slovenian government's response to my letter had seemed to prove that I could not be—and yet the few original documents I had been able to find all showed the opposite.

Folker Heinecke's story suggested an answer to this puzzle. His investigations had led him to believe that the name recorded on his Lebensborn papers might not be genuine, and that the birthplace they showed might also be false. The Lebensborn head office evidently went to great lengths to erase the original identity of those children stolen from the Reich's occupied territories.

He had discovered documents in the archives of the Nuremberg War Crimes Tribunal that told the story of a baby named Aleksander Litau who had been stolen from parents living in Alnova on the Crimean Peninsula. There were strong indications that Folker might have been this child; the dates matched, as did the Lebensborn homes the little boy had been shipped off to. Could I have suffered a similar fate?

Folker had ultimately run into the same bureaucratic stone wall that had defeated me: the documents he needed to confirm or disprove this theory were almost certainly somewhere in the ITS files in Bad Arolsen, but the archive was still not yet fully open. It was, he told our little group, very painful to be so close and yet still so far away from the truth.

*All I really want is to find the grave of my biological mother and father. I don't want to end up driven bitter and mad by wondering what might have happened to them. I just want to know who I was and what I might have been if things hadn't turned out the way they did.*

*I have to keep searching to find something that might lead me to who my parents really were and where they are buried. Then I will have done my duty as a son. I will have honored my real parents.*

I was determined that I, too, would keep searching and that one day I would track down my true family. Meeting the other Lebensborn children—fellow survivors of such a terrible experiment—gave me renewed strength to restart my own investigations And now I knew how—and where—to begin: Nuremberg.

There was one final conversation I needed to have before making the long drive home to Osnabrück. One of the few non-Lebensborn people in the room that day was a man called Josef Focks. I had not heard of him before, but apparently he had established a strong reputation for tracking down documents and information about families who had become separated during or after the war. For his efforts, the press had nicknamed him "the Father Finder."

I spoke with him briefly and explained my situation. I described the difficulty I had faced in getting information from official archives, and I told him about the documents I possessed showing me to have once been Erika Matko from St. Sauerbrunn and how this had been explicitly contradicted first by the Austrian authorities and then by the government of Slovenia.

Herr Focks listened and took notes; when I finished he agreed to help me. I was grateful, of course, but to be completely honest I was thinking more about the inquiries I would make in Nuremberg than what the "Father Finder" might unearth. I had no idea just how important he would be in the years that followed.

# TWELVE

# Nuremberg

*Lebensborn was responsible, amongst other things, for the kidnapping of foreign children for the purpose of Germanization . . . numerous Czech, Polish, Yugoslav and Norwegian children were taken from their parents.*

INDICTMENT, THE NUREMBERG MILITARY
TRIBUNALS, CASE 8

I T WAS SPRING 2003 by the time I set off on the five-hundred-kilometer drive south.

Nuremberg was the dark heart of National Socialism. Between 1927 and 1938 it was the city where Hitler held spectacular torchlit rallies—serried ranks of tens of thousands of supporters screaming *Sieg Heil* beneath an ocean of swastika banners, all captured for melodramatic propaganda films—and where the 1935 Race Laws that signaled the start of the Holocaust were promulgated.

To the controlling minds of the Nazi Party, the city's position at the very center of the country symbolized, in some mystical way, the connection between the Third Reich and the supposed Aryan supermen of Himmler's imagination. It was also heavily fortified—a fact that made it one of the last cities to fall to the Allied forces in the last weeks of the war. Despite systematic bombing that destroyed 90 percent of the medieval center, it was captured only after four days of fierce house-to-house fighting.

The three main Allied Powers had long planned to mount public trials of the Nazi leaders. On November 1, 1943, the Soviet Union, the United Kingdom, and the United States published a joint "Declaration on German Atrocities in Occupied Europe," which gave "full warning" that as and when the Nazis were defeated, the Allies would *pursue them to the uttermost ends of the earth . . . in order that justice may be done . . ."*

For the next eighteen months, as their armies slowly inched their way to victory, lawyers and politicians from all three countries hammered out a set of innovative legal principles under which Hitler and his henchmen could be prosecuted for war crimes and crimes against humanity. When the war ended the only remaining question was where to hold the hearings.

Leipzig and Luxembourg were briefly considered and rejected. The Soviet Union favored Berlin—"the capital of the fascist conspirators"— as a suitably symbolic location, but the overwhelming destruction suffered by the city made it impractical. The decision to choose Nuremberg was based on two key factors. Its role in the Nazi propaganda machine made it an appropriate site to dispense exemplary justice; but more importantly, its spacious Palace of Justice had survived the war largely intact—and its buildings included a large prison facility.

The surviving leaders of the Third Reich were brought to the cells beneath the courtroom in November 1945. Hitler himself had cheated justice, committing suicide in the *Führerbunker* amid the flames and ruins of Berlin. Himmler, too, had taken the coward's way out, swallowing a cyanide capsule while in captivity. But twenty-two others— including Reichsmarschall Hermann Göring and Deputy Führer Rudolf Hess—were brought before the International Military Tribunal and arraigned for the crimes of the Nazi regime. Eleven months later the judges—one each from France, Britain, America, and the Soviet Union—pronounced the verdicts. Twelve of the accused were sentenced to death, seven received prison sentences ranging from ten years to life in prison, and three were acquitted (two trials did not proceed, one defendant having killed himself and another was declared unfit for trial). On October 16, 1946, the executions were carried out in a gymnasium attached to the court building.

It was to this forbidding complex that I was heading that spring morning in 2003. The reason for my journey was not the famous trial itself, but a much less celebrated set of proceedings held in the same building.

Although the Allies had initially planned to hold a lengthy series of joint-power tribunals, the looming Cold War and the freeze in relations between East and West made this impossible. And so, while the main trial was still in progress, the United States made a unilateral decision to mount subsequent hearings for so-called second-tier Nazis on its own.

The result was a series of twelve separate prosecutions, between 1946 and 1949, in which a total of 183 defendants were indicted. Among them were the leaders of Lebensborn.

WITHIN DAYS OF returning home from Hadamar I had written to the office that kept records of the Nuremberg Tribunals. Given my previous experience of German official archives, I was not expecting a speedy response; and so I was pleasantly surprised to receive a letter from the archivists that said that there was an entire boxful of relevant documents and asked whether I would like to examine them.

The papers turned out to be from Case 8 of the subsequent prosecutions. This was formally titled *The United States of America v. Ulrich Greifelt et al*, but was more usually referred to as the RuSHA trial, since all fourteen defendants had held senior positions in the

Rasse und Siedlungshauptamt (RuSHA)—the Race and Settlement Main Office Himmler had established to safeguard the "racial purity" of the SS—and had then gone on to administer Lebensborn.

I began by examining the official indictment, served on March 10, 1948. It was long and detailed—fourteen closely typed foolscap pages setting out charges under three separate headings: crimes against humanity, war crimes, and membership in the SS, which had been declared a criminal organization. It started with a bleak, uncompromising assertion:

> *Between September 1939 and April 1945, all the defendants herein committed Crimes Against Humanity . . . The object of this program was to strengthen the German nation and the so-called "Aryan" race . . .*
>
> *The SS Main Race and Settlement Office (RuSHA) was responsible, amongst other things, for racial examinations. These racial examinations were carried out by RuS leaders . . . or their staff members called racial examiners (Eignungsprüfer) in connection with . . . [the] kidnapping of children eligible for Germanization . . . Lebensborn was responsible, among other things, for the kidnapping of foreign children for the purpose of Germanization.*

It was chilling to read these words; here in the cold legal language of a trial was the essence of the organization that had cared for me—if that was the right word—in my earliest years. And the indictment went on to set out both the motivation for the program and the countries in which it had operated.

> *An extensive plan of kidnapping "racially valuable" alien children was instituted. This plan had the two-fold purpose of weakening*

*enemy nations and increasing the population of Germany. It was also used as a method of retaliation and intimidation in occupied countries.*

*During the war years numerous Czech, Polish, Yugoslavian and Norwegian children were taken from their parents or guardians and classified according to their "racial value."*

I made a note of the countries identified in the charges; since the documents I had found among Gisela's papers indicated that I had been brought to the Reich for Germanization, it seemed likely that I had originally come from Czechoslovakia, Poland, Yugoslavia, or Norway—though I somehow doubted the last was a real possibility. Perhaps there would be more solid clues in the rest of the papers in the Case 8 trial folder.

But before I could get to them, the list of defendants' names suddenly caught my attention. Four senior officials of Lebensborn—three men and one woman—had been in the dock at Nuremberg, their roles and ranks spelled out clearly.

*MAX SOLLMAN—Standartenführer (Colonel) in the SS; Chief of Lebensborn.*

*GREGOR EBNER—Oberführer (Senior Colonel) in the SS. Chief of the main health department of Lebensborn.*

*INGE VIERMITZ—Deputy Chief of Main Department A of Lebensborn.*

But it was the fourth name that stopped me in my tracks.

*GUNTHER TESCH—Sturmbannführer (Major) in the SS; Chief of the Main Legal Department of Lebensborn.*

I knew that name: Sturmbannführer Tesch had signed the document that recorded the contract under which I had been handed over to Hermann and Gisela von Oelhafen. The same man who had arranged my fostering had been accused of involvement with a criminal plan to kidnap children from countries occupied by Hitler's armies. It was not a comforting revelation.

I turned back to the box of papers in front of me; it was disconcertingly large. The trial had lasted fifty-seven days, examined almost two thousand exhibits, and heard evidence from 116 witnesses for either prosecution or defense; the printed record ran to a staggering 4,780 pages. I began to wonder whether the three days I had planned to spend in Nuremberg would be enough.

The chief prosecutor, an American military lawyer named Telford Taylor, began by laying out the background to the charges. Just as I had learned in Hadamar, from the start Lebensborn's kidnapping and Germanization program had been an integral part of the Nazis' plan to eradicate those they regarded as "lesser races."

> *With the launching of the wars of aggression by the Third Reich, it became possible to put these noxious principles into practice. By the middle of 1940, a very definite plan was being effectuated. This is shown by the top secret document which Himmler wrote, entitled "Reflections on The Treatment of Peoples of Alien Races in the East"...*

I had never heard of this document—but then as Brigadier General Taylor went on to tell the court, it was so secret that Himmler gave instructions that it was not to be copied or shown to anyone beyond a small inner circle of Hitler and the most senior party leaders. After quoting a section in which the *Reichsführer* pronounced his hope that *"the concept of Jews will be completely extinguished,"* Taylor read into the trial record a section of Himmler's blueprint for stealing children deemed by his racial examiners to be pure Aryan children.

> *The parents of such children of good blood will be given the choice to give away their child—they will then probably produce no more children so that the danger of this sub-human people of the East obtaining a class of leaders, which, since it would be equal to us, would also be dangerous for us, will disappear . . .*
>
> *If we acknowledge such a child as of our blood, the parents will be notified that the child will be sent to a school in Germany and that it will remain permanently in Germany.*

Poland was the first country overrun by the Nazis. It became a testing ground for Himmler's kidnapping scheme. The court was shown a letter, dated June 18, 1941, in which he unambiguously spelled out his instructions.

> *I would consider it right if small children of Polish families who show especially good racial characteristics were apprehended and educated by us in special children's institutions and children's homes which must not be too large.*
>
> *After half a year the genealogical tree and documents of descent of those children who prove to be acceptable should be procured. After altogether one year it should be considered to give such children as foster children to childless families of good race.*

Six months later Himmler issued a new decree detailing how the kidnapping was to work in practice—and how the wheat of prospective "racially valuable" children was to be separated from the chaff of their parents—many of whom, he recognized, would be active opponents of the Nazi occupation.

> *Politically heavily incriminated persons will not be included in the resettlement action* [the Reichsführer's euphemism for wholesale stealing of children].
>
> *Their names are also to be submitted by the Higher SS and Police Leaders to the competent State Police Main Office for the purpose of transfer to a concentration camp . . . In such cases the children are to be separated from their parents . . .*
>
> *The Higher SS and Police Leaders are to pay particular attention that the Germanization of the children does not suffer as the result of detrimental influence by the parents.*
>
> *Should such detrimental influence be determined to exist, and should it be impossible to eliminate* [it] *through coercive measures by the State Police, accommodations are to be found for the children with families who are politically and ideologically above reproach and ready to take in the children as wards, without reservation and out of love for the good blood present in the children and to treat them as their own children.*

There it was: the blueprint for the Lebensborn program. It was unsettling to read such callous and twisted orders; but there was more—and worse—to come. Included in the trial record were Himmler's directives on the fate of individual Polish families who did not meet the Nazis' standards for racial "value."

> *Brunhilde Muszynski is to be taken into protective custody. Her two children, aged 4 and 7 years, are to be sterilized and lodged somewhere with foster parents.*

*Ingeborg von Avenarius is also to be taken into protective custody. Her children too are to be lodged somewhere with foster parents, after sterilization.*

There was also evidence of the justification—such as it was—for this horrific plan. The court was presented with the transcript of a speech Himmler gave in October 1943.

*I consider that in dealing with members of a foreign country, especially some Slav nationality, we must not start from German points of view and we must not endow these people with decent German thoughts and logical conclusions of which they are not capable, but we must take them as they really are.*

*Obviously in such a mixture of peoples there will always be some racially good types. Therefore I think that it is our duty to take their children with us, to remove them from their environment, if necessary by robbing or stealing them. Either we win over any good blood that we can use for ourselves, and give it a place in our people, or we destroy this blood.*

And so the children of Poland—the blond, blue-eyed ones who conformed to the Nazis' belief in "good Aryan characteristics"—were snatched from their families and transported to holding camps. Here, trained "racial examiners" set up offices to measure, prod, and evaluate thousands of youngsters brought to them by the SS. Their assessment was final and unchallengeable. A ruling issued by RuSHA explicitly stated:

*The racial sentence once passed . . . by an expert may not be altered by any office. The judgment of an expert is an expert diagnosis just like that of a physician.*

The lucky ones—if that is what they were—were then handed over to Lebensborn. In the box of files there were records, closely typed sheafs of paper recording the names of those taken from their families and shipped to the network of Lebensborn homes across Germany. I closed my eyes and imagined the scene: railway stations crowded with thousands of unaccompanied children, stuffed like cattle into trucks and carriages. Would they be crying? Who would care for them on the journey?

AND THEN—STRANGELY—A FRAGMENT of memory came to me, one I had never experienced before and yet that somehow I felt to be true. I was young, very young: I was on a train, sitting on the floor together with another small child. We were sharing a blanket, each of us trying to pull it from the other. I lost the struggle, and as the train plowed on through long, dark tunnels, I felt terribly cold. Had I been on one of the transports to Germany from the east? Had reading the accounts of what had happened in Poland awakened a recollection that had lain dormant in my subconscious for sixty years? Was this even possible?

Certainly, the more I read in the Nuremberg files the more uneasy and unsettled I felt. In my mind's eye I saw the trial unfolding, its focus now shifting from Poland to a little village in what was then Czechoslovakia.

Marie Doležalová was fifteen when she stood on the witness stand in 1947 and gave testimony about what had happened to her five years earlier. On the morning of June 9, 1942, ten trucks filled with SS and Gestapo troops rolled into Lidice, a farming hamlet near Prague.

Two weeks earlier Czech partisans had assassinated SS-Obergruppenführer Reinhard Heydrich, Himmler's protégé and the man charged with ruling this corner of the Reich's conquered lands.

Hitler demanded mass reprisals; the raid on Lidice was specifically ordered because the village was suspected of having links to the men who killed Heydrich.

Armed soldiers jumped out of their vehicles and rounded up the entire population. Every adult man—173 of them, including Marie's father—was lined up and shot against the wall of a barn. Their bodies were laid out in seventeen rows in an orchard, before the village was burned to the ground.

The women of the village—almost two hundred of them, some heavily pregnant, were transported to Ravensbrück concentration camp. Their children were snatched from them; 184 youngsters were pushed into buses and transported to a former textile factory in Łodz. By order of Himmler's staff they were not fed, and were forced to sleep on cold dirt floors without blankets.

And then RuSHA's "race examiners" arrived. Every child was assessed for signs of Aryan qualities. They "failed" 103 children: of them 74 were immediately handed over to the Gestapo. It had them transported to the extermination camp at Chelmno, seventy kilometers away. Here they were gassed to death in specially adapted killing trucks.

Just seven children were selected as suitable for Germanization. Marie Doležalová was one of them.

When she arrived at the children's home, she found herself among many other children from different countries. She was forced to learn German and was punished if she was caught speaking Czech. Lebensborn eventually handed her over to an approved German family; although her foster parents were kind, giving her two new dresses to mark her arrival with them, she was gradually made to forget where she had come from.

After the war ended, the handful of Lidice women who had survived the massacre and the concentration camp began searching for their missing children. A year later—just before she gave evidence at

Nuremberg—Marie was reunited with her mother, who was by then dying. But as she stood by her mother's bedside she realized that she now couldn't remember a word of her native language.

All of this Marie Doležalová told the judges at Nuremberg. As I read her testimony, I put myself in her place. Had I, like her, come from a village burned to the ground by Himmler's troops? Had I been one of the "racially valuable" lucky ones—saved from the death camps by a glimpse of blond hair or the hint of blue eyes? If so, where exactly had I been stolen from? And was there any hope that, like Marie, I might one day meet my real mother before she died?

And then I found the lists.

They were tattered gray sheets of foolscap, prepared by Lebensborn staff in 1944, and almost sixty years later the type had faded, making them only just legible. Each was divided into four columns; the first was an alphabetical list of names, and since the adjacent column showed birth dates—all from the early 1940s—it was clear that this was some kind of register of children. The third column was headed "transferred to," and next to each entry was a date. There were 473 children identified in these documents. Halfway down one I read the following:

*Matko, Erika.*

[Born on] *11.11.41.*

[Transferred to] *Oberst Hermann von Oelhafen, Munich, Gentzstrasse 5*

[On] *3.6.44*

I had found my name—my original identity. I knew that it had to be genuine; not only were these official court records, but the address shown for Hermann—and the date on which I was handed over to him—were correct. I sat back with the document in front of me. I was surprised to find that I was not emotional; ever since I had received the letter from the Slovenian government telling me that I could not be Erika Matko—because that person was still living in the Rogaška Slatina area—I had felt lost and unsure of who I really was. Now, as I looked at this fading Lebensborn list, I felt my identity coming back to me. I felt once again that I was—or had once been—Erika Matko.

But where had she—or rather, I—come from? I discovered that accompanying the lists were two sworn statements by former Lebensborn staff who had been interrogated by investigators for the Nuremberg prosecutors. The first was a woman called Maria-Martha Heinze-Wissede, who had worked in the Lebensborn head office. On August 9, 1948, she had been shown the documents and identified the origin of some of the children. Erika Matko was one of them.

*From the lists before me, I recognized the following names of Yugoslavian children . . .*

*. . . Erika MATKO*

*These children, I know only their files a little, since they had already been transferred to . . . German families by Lebensborn. As was clear from the documents, they were called "bandit children," and Lebensborn took them over from Volksdeutsche Mittelstelle (VoMi) . . . As far as I remember, the Lebensborn took these children from a Volksdeutsche Mittelstelle camp in the district of Bayreuth.*

And now my heart raced. There it was in black and white: I had definitely been brought from Yugoslavia and handed to Lebensborn by this VoMi organization.

A quick search showed this to have been another of the confusing and overlapping bodies answering to Himmler; it was set up before the war, ostensibly to manage the interests of the *Volksdeutsche*—ethnic Germans who lived outside the borders of Nazi Germany. But once Hitler's armies overran Poland, Czechoslovakia, and Yugoslavia, VoMi settled half a million German volunteers in the conquered territories, simultaneously shipping out or imprisoning the rightful occupants. It was essentially a precursor to what we now call ethnic cleansing—and the organization's involvement in my origins did not bode well for the fate of my biological family.

Who were they? There was a clue—a thrilling hint—in the affidavit of Maria-Martha Heinze-Wissede: I and the other Yugoslavian youngsters were listed as "bandit children." In Nazi terminology this meant partisan fighters. I felt a surge of very real pride; our fathers were rebels—they had opposed the Nazi occupiers. How brave they must have been. I honestly doubted that in their position I would have found the courage to fight back against Hitler's armies.

The second witness statement was from a former Lebensborn clerk called Emilie Edelmann. She had joined the organization in 1939 and worked within it until the very end, rising to a position that gave her responsibility for the care of children being readied for placement with foster families. On April 3, 1948, she, too, told her American interrogators that children had been snatched from Yugoslavia—and filled in a few of the missing details of my journey to a Lebensborn home. She described these kidnapped children as *Südost-kinder*—VoMi-speak for those taken from the southeastern territories conquered by Germany.

I reread the documents to be certain, but in the end it was unequivocal: the information in the Nuremberg files was definitive proof that I had been one of at least twenty-five infants—children of brave resistance fighters—who in 1942 and 1943 were kidnapped and transported from Yugoslavia to the Fatherland for Germanization.

I had been taken to a VoMi holding camp at Werdenfels in southern Germany before being shipped on to the Sonnenwiese home at Kohren-Sahlis and then eventually given to "the family von Oelhafen, Munich."

I was, I think, a little stunned. I had been shipped from place to place like a human parcel before being handed over to an organization that masqueraded as a humanitarian provider of maternity homes but was, in reality, cynically dealing in stolen babies.

I had only one question left to answer before I left Nuremberg: How did the trial end—and what punishment was meted out to the senior Lebensborn officials in the dock?

I was astonished to discover that although most of the top RuSHA officials had been convicted and sentenced to lengthy terms in prison, the four Lebensborn defendants had been acquitted of crimes against humanity and war crimes. The three men had been found guilty of membership in the SS—as a woman, Inge Viermitz was excluded from its ranks—but none spent a single additional day behind bars. Despite all the evidence presented to them, the judges had reached the incredible conclusion that Lebensborn had really been no more than "a welfare organization."

I was furious; I had read the same evidence, but I had also listened to the harrowing accounts from my fellow survivors at the meeting in Hadamar. I knew the truth now—and it made me more determined than ever to discover how I had fallen into Lebensborn's clutches.

I knew now that whatever the government of Slovenia thought, I had definitely come from there. The only questions were how to prove it—and what I would find if I did.

# THIRTEEN

# Rogaška Slatina

*I would be very, very grateful if you could answer some questions about your childhood . . . I am not asking out of mere curiosity . . .*

LETTER TO ERIKA MATKO,
*June 2003*

I FOUND A LARGE number of people throughout Germany with the surname "Matko." I wrote to every one of their addresses, asking if they knew anything about my background or that of Hermann and Gisela von Oelhafen. It was no more than a succession of shots in the dark, and I did not hold out much hope that I would receive any replies. To my surprise letters began trickling back; each thanked me for contacting them and wished me well, but none were able to help me with my investigation.

In the meantime, the Father Finder was busy. He was not deterred by the results of my letters to the German Matkos; out of the goodness of his heart, he expanded his geographical search.

Josef Focks is one of the people without whom I would never have found the truth about my past. He was a former army officer who had been seconded to NATO in the 1980s.

During a posting to Norway he first encountered the stories of children fathered by German troops and the plight of those who had been born in the Lebensborn program. Moved by their pain—and the sense of shame that had blighted their lives—he agreed to help them track down their families.

From the outset, he ran into the problem caused by Lebensborn's deliberate withholding of many of the fathers' names. Ironically, it was the logistical difficulties affecting any genealogical search in the days before the Internet and online records that led him to find innovative ways round the impasse. He made—and made use of—local contacts (he found that taxi drivers were good sources of information), dug into obscure archives and the libraries of old newspapers, and even visited cemeteries to examine the names carved into headstones. Gradually, he developed a way to solve the puzzle.

By the time I met him he had taken on more than a thousand individual cases—not all of them Lebensborn children—successfully tracing family members in most of them. His investigations had led him across Germany and as far afield as America and Australia, and his office in Bonn was stuffed with innumerable files, each one bulging with paper. All of this he did voluntarily and without charging a penny for his time; he had long since retired from the army and lived on his state pension, helping people like me for nothing more than the reward of easing our pain. I cannot thank him enough.

It was Josef who first found the most promising Matkos. He had gotten in touch with one of his contacts, a woman whose mother had been taken from Yugoslavia by the Nazis as slave labor; with her help he discovered the contact details for several Matkos still living in or near Rogaška Slatina.

They seemed to be an extended family; some were my age or slightly older, others clearly a generation younger. Most promising of all, one of them was named Erika.

Josef unearthed an address for her and also found the telephone number for a Maria Matko, who, he thought, might be related. We agreed that he would phone Maria and that I would write to Erika.

I sat down at the computer and thought about what I should say. It was not an easy letter to compose. I knew nothing about this woman, nor anything about the country in which she lived. In the end I decided to speak openly and from the heart of my need to discover the truth about my past, and to hope that somehow this would touch her enough to respond. I told myself that since many of the unrelated Matkos in Germany who I had contacted out of the blue had taken the trouble to reply even though they could not help me, perhaps this person bearing my name, and who lived in the place I knew I came from, might also be moved by my plea for help.

*Osnabrück, Germany*
*February 16, 2003*

*Dear Mrs. Matko*

*I am writing to you today about a very personal matter and hope that you can help me. The problem of course is that I do not speak Slovenian and I cannot hope that you speak German. But I hope that there is somebody who can help you to translate my letter.*

*For some years I have been researching my biological parents, and during this research I found out very strange things, which have made me very anxious and disturbed, but I know that I must keep going on.*

*My foster parents picked me up from the Lebensborn home "Sonnenwiese." There I was given two vaccination documents in which my name is shown as Erika Matko, born in*

*St. Sauerbrunn. I don't have any other documentation about my early life. I don't know the circumstances which brought me to the home. My foster parents didn't give me any information.*

*Ten years ago I didn't even know that I was a Lebensborn child. The Red Cross couldn't find out any information about my identity. I asked Dr. Georg Lilienthal, who is a researcher about Lebensborn and has published a book about the subject.*

*He gave me the idea that maybe I'm a member of the group of kidnapped children, and my origins lie in Yugoslavia.*

*Now in the course of my research I have discovered you. I don't ask from curiosity but I only want to know how this double identity has occurred. Did you ever live in a Lebensborn home or were you lucky enough to spend your whole life in Rogaška Slatina?*

*I would be very, very grateful if you could answer my questions about your childhood.*

> *Best wishes,*
> *Ingrid von Oelhafen*

There was nothing more I could say or do. I mailed the letter, hoping that something in it would strike a chord with this other Erika Matko.

In the meantime, Josef Focks had made progress. He had made contact with Maria Matko and they had a good conversation via phone with the help of a translator, as he didn't speak Slovenian and she could not understand German. She was, apparently, my age and had spent her whole life in Rogaška Slatina.

From what Maria told Josef, she was the matriarch of the extended Matko family, which had once been involved with the anti-Nazi partisan movement. She was slightly hazy on the details, remembering only that the Nazis had executed one member of the family and that she had heard a story, long ago, that three children might have been kidnapped in the early 1940s.

It sounded tantalizingly close to the likely history of the Matkos that I was looking for, but even more promising was the news that she knew the mysterious Erika very well.

But it was the final piece of information that threw me. Herr Focks had persuaded Maria that she should meet me—and that she should bring Erika with her. I was instantly nervous; I wanted desperately to go, but the prospect terrified me. What if these were the "wrong" Matkos, and my journey turned out to be a wild-goose chase? I would, I knew, be devastated. Even worse, even if this Maria and Erika were my relatives, perhaps they would be hostile or somehow resent me.

But the Father Finder was having none of it. He pushed and pushed until I agreed to his plan. This involved flying first to Munich then on to Ljubljana, the Slovenian capital. From here I would have to find a taxi to take me the eighty kilometers to the main town in the region, Celje.

There was an additional reason for going to the country. Every autumn a handful of survivors of the Nazis' kidnapping and deportation program meet in Celje. Josef had arranged for me to join them before heading on the next day to Rogaška Slatina, where I was to meet Maria in a café. Nor was I to go alone; he had asked a friend of his who spoke Slovenian to accompany me and be my translator.

As the date for my departure approached I realized that I knew precious little about Slovenia or its history. I didn't even know how the country had come into being after the breakup of Yugoslavia. What I discovered began to give me an insight into what life might have held for me had I not been stolen and placed in the Lebensborn program.

Yugoslavia had been one of the first countries to overthrow their German conquerors. Under the leadership of Josip Tito, the partisans were the most effective anti-Nazi resistance force in occupied Europe; by the middle of 1943 their activity had grown from sporadic guerrilla raids to major military victories, during which they had inflicted heavy casualties that Hitler's army could ill afford. By the start of 1944 they had managed to push the Wehrmacht out of the Serbian regions. A year later all German troops were expelled.

They achieved this with only limited support from the Soviet Union, and although Tito's postwar regime was unashamedly Communist— a single-party state with little tolerance of dissent or democracy, for the next twenty-five years the country was the most independent of all the Soviet Union's satellites behind the Iron Curtain. It began to distance itself from Moscow in 1948, determined to forge its own brand of socialism.

It felt free to criticize the Kremlin and the West in equal measure, and was one of the founders of the Non-Aligned Movement—the group of states that defiantly refused to ally themselves with either side in the Cold War.

But there were always tensions beneath the surface. The new nation had been welded together from six separate and frequently hostile republics: Serbia, Croatia, Bosnia-Herzegovina, Macedonia, Montenegro, and Slovenia. Each of these had very different ethnic, religious, and political histories. What held them together was the inspirational figure of Josip Tito. His death in 1980 started an unraveling of the whole country.

Serbs had always been the largest ethnic group in Yugoslavia, and prior to the Second World War had been the most dominant force in the Kingdom of Yugoslavia. With Tito gone, Serbian Communist leader Slobodan Milošević sought to restore this historic supremacy; the other republics, especially Slovenia and Croatia, denounced this power grab but were unable to stop it.

Strikes by ethnic Albanian miners in Kosovo in 1989 were the spark that ignited the simmering tension. Slovenia and Croatia supported the Albanian miners and the strikes turned into widespread demonstrations demanding a Kosovan republic. This angered Serbia's leadership, which proceeded to use police force, and then sent in the federal army to restore order.

In January 1990 an extraordinary Congress of the League of Communists of Yugoslavia was convened. Since the country was a one-party state, this was effectively the ruling body for all of the federal republic. The meeting degenerated into an argument between Slovenia and Serbia about the future of the nation; in the end the league dissolved itself—and the writing was on the wall for the future of Yugoslavia.

The immediate outcome was a constitutional crisis; fueled by a toxic rise in ethnic-based nationalism and inspired by the fall of communism across the rest of Eastern Europe, five of the republics demanded independence and an end to Serbian dominance. The stage was set for war.

What followed was Europe's worst conflict since the Second World War—and one that once again raised the specter of crimes against humanity. Over the next decade, at least 140,000 people died in the fighting, but hundreds of thousands—possibly millions—endured ethnic cleansing, rape as a weapon of war, concentration camps, and mass bombing.

The first of these dirty wars broke out in Slovenia. In December 1990, 88 percent of the population voted for full independence from the disintegrating federal republic, knowing that to do so would inevitably lead to an attempted invasion by the Serb-dominated Yugoslav People's Army.

The local government secretly reorganized its antiquated territorial defense force, turning it into a well-trained and -equipped guerrilla army. The partisan resistance that had once driven Hitler's troops from the country was effectively reborn.

The Slovenians knew that they stood no chance in a conventional battle; the YPA was simply too big and too powerful. So the government prepared for a campaign of asymmetric warfare—a return to the resistance tactics of blowing up bridges and small close-quarter attacks in the towns and villages of their nascent nation.

At the same time the government sought help from the European community and the United States. Neither was prepared to recognize the independence of Slovenia since they found it more convenient to deal with a single federation than with a series of small states. It was a rebuff that emboldened the Serbs, and that made a full-blown civil war inevitable.

The first shot was fired, by the YPA, on June 27, 1990, in the small village of Divača, just 75 kilometers from Ljubljana. The same afternoon, Slovenian soldiers shot down two Yugoslavian army helicopters. Over the next ten days the fighting moved westward, first toward Ljubljana, then on past the capital and into the eastern heartland around Celje and Rogaška Slatina. A cease-fire was announced on July 6; Slovenia won its independence, though at the cost of at least sixty-two deaths and almost 330 wounded.

In contrast to the ensuing conflicts in Croatia, Bosnia, and Kosovo, this was a small war; but it was the first time since the Nazis had been expelled that Slovenians had their freedom. In some slightly inexplicable way I felt proud.

At the end of September 2003 I flew to Munich. Josef Focks had arranged for me to meet his translator at the airport so we could fly on to Ljubljana together. But by the time our flight was called, he had not arrived. I had no choice but to get on board alone. I was already nervous about who or what I would find in Slovenia, and since I spoke only German, I felt vulnerable and exposed. Fortunately, the translator managed to get a message to the plane and asked the flight attendant to tell me that he had been held up in traffic and would catch a later flight and meet me at Ljubljana.

I waited all day in the airport with no sign of the translator. I had no signal on my cell phone, no one seemed to speak German, and I could not figure out how to use the local pay phones. All I could do was sit and hope that my contact would turn up.

By the time he finally arrived, it was midevening and I was in something of a state. But I had no time to dwell on my feelings; there was to be a meeting of the stolen Slovenian children that evening in the primary school at Celje. This town, I gathered, had been called Cilli during the German occupation, and had been both a center for partisan resistance and the site of Nazi reprisals.

As we drove through the countryside I looked out of the car window, trying to take in the landscape of what I knew to be the land of my birth. I had wondered if seeing it for the first time in almost seventy years would prompt some memories. I was disappointed to find that it did not.

I had little or no idea about who would be at the meeting, or whether the people there would help me uncover the truth about my past. I was, therefore, surprised to discover that the event in Celje that evening was very far from the first gathering of stolen children. They had started searching for one another as far back as 1962, determined to tell their stories to the (then) Yugoslavian public.

The men and women I met that evening were all in their

eighties—between ten and fifteen years older than me. They were the leaders of what had become an officially supported group of survivors, and their accounts filled in some of the gaps in my knowledge.

Throughout 1942 a total of 654 children—from babies to eighteen-year-olds—were snatched from their families by the Nazis and shipped off to a succession of camps across the Reich. Most of the older ones—at least those that survived the rigors of slave labor or attempted Germanization—had been brought back home at the end of the war. By the time I arrived in Celje only around 200 were still alive.

Despite their age, their memories were strong and they were determined that the world should not forget what had been done to them. Two speakers stood up in the primary school to give testimony. I sat silently; even if I had felt able to trust the translator to speak for me, I knew too little to make any worthwhile contribution.

But my presence had been noted. At the end of the meeting, three people came over to speak to me; each had been stolen from Celje in August 1942, and to my complete astonishment, each one said they recognized me.

The first was a woman. She was seventeen when she was caught in a roundup of children from the area and held for two days in the primary school by SS troops. The children were aged between infancy and eighteen years old; because they were separated from their mothers, the older ones were ordered to look after the babies. This warm and emotional elderly woman told me that the babies were constantly crying; her task had been to clean the smallest ones—and that she specifically remembered washing me.

I couldn't believe what I was hearing. I would have been less than a year old when the roundup happened; how on earth could someone recognize me more than sixty years later? But somehow this woman believed that she did. It was astonishing.

I had come to Slovenia unsure of who I really was and hoping only to find some evidence that tied me to the country. Instead, I had come face-to-face with someone who could place me in Celje on the day that I was stolen—and who had actually held and looked after me when I was a baby. On reflection it seemed more probable that the woman had been told I was coming and this had prompted her to remember me. But either way it was a connection.

The next person I spoke to was a man around the same age. He had been fourteen on the day of the kidnapping, and he was able to tell me a bit more about what had happened to the stolen children on the day after the roundup. He told me that we were transported 150 kilometers north to the holding camp at Frohnleiten in Austria. What's more, he was adamant that he had seen me there—and that the name he knew me by was Erika Matko.

A third person chimed in, another elderly lady who wanted to confirm what the man said. She, too, had been kidnapped from Celje and shipped to Frohnleiten, and she, too, remembered me there and that my name was Erika Matko.

I suddenly felt intensely happy. After so long, so many disappointments, I had firsthand evidence of who I once had been and where I had come from. It was an extraordinary feeling.

I did not have time to press my new contacts for details of the kidnapping. Each told me only that they had known me, that I was one of them, before it was time to leave. I would have to wait to find out more about the events of August 1942 and how I had been caught up in them.

From Celje we moved on to the Maribor region. Ahead of my meeting with Maria, Josef Focks had arranged for me to meet two people whose surname was Matko. He had also equipped me with sterile test tubes and cotton swabs so that if these Matkos were willing I could take samples of their saliva, which we would later have analyzed to see if I shared any genetic similarities. In this way I would discover whether we were related.

Our first stop was a village near Rogaška Slatina. As we drove in I looked around to see if the landscape prompted any memories; it didn't. The village was clearly very poor; the woman I was due to meet was eighty years old and living with her forty-year-old son. Both seemed puzzled by my visit, but the old lady agreed to give me a saliva sample. Her son was slightly more hostile and refused. Neither of them was able to tell me much about their family background and I came to the conclusion that if we were related it was probably only distantly.

The next Matko was a thirty-year-old hairdresser. She, too, willingly gave me a sample for DNA analysis, but again had little information to help me on my journey.

Finally it was time for the meeting with Maria Matko. Herr Focks had arranged our rendezvous in a little café in Rogaška Slatina, and she had promised to bring the mysterious other Erika with her. But the moment I walked in I could see that Maria was alone. I felt a sharp pang of disappointment.

But Maria herself turned out to be warm, helpful, and a vital link in unlocking the chains of my past. She was seventy-three years old, not a Matko by birth, but had married into the family. Her husband was named Ludvig and he had two sisters: Tanja, who was older than he and Erika, who was younger. Both Ludvig and Tanja were dead but Erika was still alive, if rather infirm; she was the one to whom I had written and who was supposed to have come to the café, but Maria said she had been unwilling to meet me.

It was plain from our conversation that none of the extended Matko family thought I was related to them. Maria was the most open-minded, but even she was skeptical. And at that point I was beginning to share their doubts.

But then Maria gave me some details that once again raised my hopes. The parents of Ludvig, Tanja, and Erika had been called Johann and Helena—the very names that I had been given three years before by the archivist in Maribor. What's more, Johann had been imprisoned by the Nazis for resistance activity; that seemed to fit what Georg Lilienthal had told me about my background.

Over the preceding years there had been a pattern to all my attempts to discover the truth. One piece of new information would emerge to lift my spirits and make me believe that I could discover where I came from. But it would always be followed by a letter or a conversation that dashed those hopes and sent me back into despair. And so it proved that day in Rogaška Slatina; no sooner had my expectations been raised than they were lowered once again. Maria produced two photographs; one was of Helena, taken in 1964. She was looking directly at the camera, a solid-looking woman, with dark hair and a strong but kindly face. The second picture was of Erika; my immediate reaction was that she looked just like Helena. That suggested she was Helena's daughter—and, if so, it meant that I could not have been.

When we parted I was a little depressed. The only thing that buoyed my spirits was that Maria agreed to meet me again—and told me that she would talk to the other members of the Matko family to see if they would cooperate with me.

The next day I went to her apartment. She was babysitting her granddaughter but talked openly about the family history. She told me that Ludvig, Tanja, and Erika had lived with their mother and father until he was arrested by the Nazis for resistance activity and imprisoned in a concentration camp. He had, though, been released and returned to the family home in the early summer of 1942—after which her knowledge ended.

Johann's brother, Ignaz, had not been so lucky; he, too, was a partisan and arrested by the Germans, but he was shot by a firing squad.

During our conversation Maria's son, Rafael, joined us. He was in his forties, solidly built, and balding. Although he was polite he clearly did not believe I was related to them. It was obvious that the family was close-knit and protective of one another.

The exception to this was, apparently, Erika. Maria told me that her sister-in-law had never married (though she did have a son) and had been so ill throughout her life that she had never worked. It was plain that for all the family bonds—Erika was usually invited to Sunday lunches—the two women weren't particularly close.

By the time I took my leave, I had, I think, convinced myself that although this family seemed to share remarkable similarities to the Matkos I was searching for, they were probably not my blood family. Nonetheless, before I set off I explained about my DNA testing plans. Rafael kindly agreed to give me a saliva sample, and, after some hesitation, so did his cousin Marko.

My final appointment was in Maribor. I went to a museum that maintained a special section dedicated to the remembrance of what the Nazis had done in Slovenia.

In addition to rounding up and executing "bandits"—partisan fighters like Ignaz Matko—all Slovenian books were burned, the language was banned, and anyone caught speaking it was severely punished. Himmler's plan to subjugate the local population and treat them no better than cattle was put into effect brutally and efficiently.

I cannot in all honesty say that I was deeply shocked by what I saw and heard in the museum. Once perhaps I would have been; but everything I had learned over the previous three years about Lebensborn and its operations overshadowed the routine cruelty of the Nazi occupation. I was also preoccupied with what I had discovered about my own past during my four days in Slovenia. I had arrived in the country uncertain about how I fit into its history in general and into the story of the Matko family in particular. With each contradictory new piece of information I had, by turns, been convinced that I was Erika Matko from Rogaška Slatina and then absolutely certain that I could not be her. By the time I got back on the plane in Ljubljana, I was completely confused.

In the end I decided that I had been away from my life and my physiotherapy practice in Osnabrück for too long. My patients needed me, and I needed them. It was time to go home, time to be Ingrid von Oelhafen once again.

# FOURTEEN

# Blood

*Scientific analysis is 93.3 per cent certain...*

DNA TEST RESULTS,
*October 2003*

How do we put together the jigsaw puzzle of our lives? How do we find the right shapes and make them fit together so that they form an image we can recognize? It is not easy even when all the pieces are assembled in front of us and we have the picture on the box to compare it with. How much harder when we lack the solid, clear-cut corners to build out from.

This was how the story of my birth and childhood looked to me when I arrived home from Slovenia. I had dozens of individual pieces, but they were oddly shaped, sometimes overlapping, sometimes con-tradictory. There seemed to be no way to make them interlock and reveal the true picture.

Were the survivors of the Celje kidnappings right that I was the Erika Matko they remembered? Could it even be possible that some-one would recognize in the face of a seventy-two-year-old woman the features of a nine-month-old baby they had known only in the most traumatic of circumstances? They seemed so certain, but their accounts were at odds with the reactions of Maria Matko and her son; they plainly did not believe I was part of their family.

And always in the background was the shadowy figure of the other Erika; she had still not replied to my letter and had deliberately avoided meeting me in Rogaška Slatina. How was I to assemble such conflicting pieces into a complete and convincing jigsaw puzzle?

The answer, I hoped, lay in the little swabs and test tubes I had brought home with me. Saliva analysis would provide genetic fingerprints that were as reliable as a blood test in determining family relationships. The irony of this was not lost on me. The Lebensborn experiment had been based on the Nazis' belief in blood as the determining factor of human worth. Himmler's obsession with blood and bloodlines was the reason I had been plucked from my family—whoever they were—in Yugoslavia and reborn as a German child. It had shaped the course of my life from that day onward. Now I was trying to use it to unravel the tangled web Lebensborn had spun.

The saliva swabs had not been given without a great deal of anxiety. There had been a dispute within the Matko family about my having them; some of the younger members of the family had been adamantly opposed to the whole idea of scientific tests to establish whether I was one of them. They worried, I think, primarily about the stress this could cause to Erika, who was not in good health.

Others, though, believed that the results could be the vital piece of the puzzle; and after much discussion I had been given the Matkos' blessing to have their samples analyzed. I set about finding a laboratory that would test them for me.

I discovered that it was not going to be easy—or cheap. The science of DNA testing began only in 1985 and was then both rudimentary and the exclusive domain of law enforcement agencies. Although it had since been refined and made more commercially available, it was still expensive. I had to provide my own saliva for comparison and faced a bill of at least one thousand euros to have my samples analyzed.

All of the cotton swabs I had collected in Slovenia would be processed so that the individual DNA of each of us could be isolated. Although 99.9 percent of human DNA sequences are the same for everyone, there are enough differences to make it possible to distinguish one individual from another. What the scientists would look for were places in these sequences called loci.

Where two people are related by blood, these loci are very similar to each other; in samples from biologically unrelated donors, they look completely different.

I DECIDED TO use my savings to pay for the tests. It would mean tightening my belt and not taking vacations for the foreseeable future, but in the end I realized that there was simply no other way to solve the puzzle. I carefully wrapped up the swabs and sent them off to the laboratory in Munich.

It took several months for the results to come back. What they revealed was both the answer to the big puzzle and a new mystery.

I looked first at the tests on the samples provided by the hairdresser and the old lady; as I had suspected, neither had any genetic relationship to me. I allowed myself a guilty feeling of slight relief; it was clear that the old lady lived in some poverty, which was sad to see. All along I had hoped that my biological family had not suffered; it was painful to imagine that my mother might have had such a hard life.

The next set of results were for Rafael Matko, the son of Ludvig and Maria. When I read them, my guilty feelings were transformed into pure happiness.

*Scientific analysis shows that Ingrid von Oelhafen and Rafael Matko are relatives in the second degree ... it is 93.3 per cent certain that Ingrid von Oelhafen is the aunt of Rafael Matko.*

There it was, the evidence I had been seeking for so long. If I was Rafael's aunt, that meant I was Ludvig's sister—and therefore the daughter of Johann and Helena Matko. I had found the vital piece of the jigsaw puzzle: I was unquestionably Erika Matko from St. Sauerbrunn/Rogaška Slatina.

It is hard for me to convey what this news meant. Unless you have lived your life as I had—haunted by never knowing who you are and where you came from—I don't think it is possible to fully understand the overwhelming elation. It was like being liberated. It felt as if the weight of sixty years had been lifted from me.

But, as always seemed to happen, the other test results dragged me back to uncertainty. Analysis of the saliva sample given by Marko Matko—Rafael's cousin—had yielded what appeared to be a completely contradictory outcome; it showed that to a 98.8 percent degree of certainty I was not related to him.

This simply didn't make sense. I looked again at the Matko family tree to remind myself of what I knew: Johann and Helena had three children, Tanja, Ludvig, and Erika. Ludvig's son was Rafael, and the tests proved that I was his aunt; therefore I must be Erika. But the same set of results showed that Tanja's son, Marko, was not my biological relative. No matter how I arranged these puzzle pieces, I could not get them to fit. If I was Ludvig and Tanja's sister, then why wasn't I Marko's aunt? The Matko family seemed to be surrounded by secrets.

The person most likely to have the answers was the mysterious other Erika. She was the last living first-degree blood relative—at least, in theory. She had been raised by Helena and Johann and grown up with Tanja and Ludvig. But she was still ignoring my letter. I had now to assume that she was not prepared to help me find the truth. It was immensely frustrating. I could not understand why she was being so obstructive.

In the end I decided to focus on the positives. I knew for certain that I was—or had once been—Erika Matko, daughter of Johann and Helena, and that Ludvig at least was my brother. Quite how Tanja and the other Erika fit into the picture was still a mystery: but at least I could be certain who my biological parents were. That was a very real comfort.

I was, though, no closer to solving the puzzle of how I had been taken from them. And it would be another four years before those pieces fell into place.

# FIFTEEN

# Pure

*To be rooted is perhaps the most important and least recognized need of the human soul.*

SIMONE WEIL,
*THE NEED FOR ROOTS, 1949*

WERNIGERODE LIES ON the eastern edge of the Harz Mountains in the German heartland of Saxony. It is a quiet, picturesque town, in which half-timbered houses flank the Holtemme River and horse-drawn carts still rumble through cobbled streets. It looks and feels like the setting for a fairy tale, the sort of place where the Brothers Grimm might have collected one of their stories.

But Wernigerode had another, altogether less cozy history. On the top of a steep hill just outside the town lie the ruins of Heim Harz, one of the network of Lebensborn homes.

It was late summer 2005. I was driving to Wernigerode to take part in the creation of a new organization. *Lebensspuren*—literally translated, this means "traces of life"—was the first attempt by those of us who had been born or reared in Himmler's master race program formally to band together; our aim was both to provide much-needed support and to begin the process of bringing Lebensborn out of the prejudice and shame that prevented public understanding of what had been done to us in its homes.

It was a long journey. The road stretched more than 260 kilometers through the woods and fields of central Germany; as I drove I had time to reflect on how I had gotten here. It was more than five years since I had begun the search for my roots. I had learned so much during them, and yet I realized I still knew relatively little.

In the ten months since I had received the scientific tests that proved who I was, I had made no real progress in discovering how I had been brought into the Lebensborn program; nor did I fully understand the extent of the experiment itself.

In this I was far from alone. The meeting in Hadamar had been a first step for the handful of Lebensborn children to come together and share our stories. Each of us had a little part of the overall puzzle, but even put together, these still could not complete the full picture. The aim of Lebensspuren was to find at least some of the elusive pieces.

The title itself was a deliberate twist on Lebensborn; where that had been, in Himmler's vision and language, the Fount of Life, our association—formally registered with the authorities—was to be the way for its survivors to explain it. But I was also aware of a possible subtle play on words contained within our chosen designation; that middle syllable, *pur*, was an acknowledgment of the Nazis' obsession with racial purity that had been at the root of our creation.

To match these founding principles we had chosen a quotation that would head our articles of association. *"Uprootedness is by far the most dangerous disease to which human society is exposed. Whoever is uprooted, uproots others. Who is rooted himself, doesn't uproot others. To be rooted is perhaps the most important and least recognized need of the human soul."*

It came from a French philosopher and activist, Simone Weil. She had fought fascism in Germany in the early 1930s and later as a volunteer on the republican side during the Spanish Civil War. In 1943 she wrote a book called *The Need for Roots*, examining the social, cultural, and spiritual malaise undermining Western society; the quotation we selected from it perfectly encapsulated the story of our lives.

I LIKED GUNTRAM Weber the moment I met him. We were staying in the same guesthouse and we also shared a common interest in working with young people. Guntram was a creative-writing teacher specializing in helping disadvantaged youngsters. He was two years younger than me, but his face bore witness to the pain he had experienced all his life. When he stood up to tell his story at our meeting, his eyes repeatedly filled with tears as he described his struggle to find the truth about his origins, and when he did, the overwhelming desire to run away from it.

He had grown up in an outwardly normal postwar German family, living with his parents and two siblings—an older sister and a younger brother. But behind closed doors it was a different story.

*As a child I remember sensing that I wasn't quite normal. Relatives seemed to treat me awkwardly and it gradually became clear that the man I called Father was actually my stepfather. Of course, I wanted to find out who my real father was, but the subject was taboo in our house.*

*Relatives had been well-drilled by my mother to hide the truth behind vague statements. "It was the war," they would say. "Things were very confusing. We didn't see much of each other— you will have to ask your mother."*

It wasn't until he was thirteen that Guntram's mother agreed to discuss the issue.

*"Well, Guntram," she said. "You are old enough to know the truth about your father now." Then she gave me a name, told me when his birthday was and that she had married him in 1938 on a beautiful sunny day and that they had driven to church in a horse-drawn cart.*

*During the war he had been a truck driver for the Luftwaffe, far away from the front, who had died driving over a land mine in Yugoslavia. She added that he certainly wasn't involved in killing anyone.*

*But there were no documents and no photos of this man, and when I pressed her, my mother said she didn't want to say any more about him because it was too painful.*

It was a plausible story. Guntram was a little suspicious, but the climate of family life in Germany during the 1950s actively discouraged awkward questions. Many children were told lies about what their parents did in the war, and as I knew from my own experience, it wasn't the "done thing" to challenge them.

Curiosity and uncertainty gnawed away at Guntram. Sometimes he thought about confronting his mother about his doubts, but he never managed to do so. The lack of any photos or documents led him to disbelieve the story of the noncombatant Luftwaffe driver; instead he began worrying that his father had been a Nazi and that this was the reason for his family's secretive behavior. He began inspecting his facial features in the mirror and poring over history books in the school library, searching for photos of soldiers that could be his father, or of women concentration camp guards who looked like his mother.

For one terrible period he even convinced himself that Josef Goebbels, Reich minister for propaganda and one of Hitler's most devoted followers, might be his father. A year or so later he made an even more disturbing discovery.

*My mother had a strongbox in the bottom right-hand corner of her wardrobe. One afternoon when she was out, I decided to look in. I had terrible qualms about doing this; I knew I was breaking the trust between us and she was my only security in the world. But I felt I had no choice.*

Inside the trunk, Guntram found the first clue to his identity: a small silver cup. It bore a profoundly unsettling inscription.

*We were a fairly poor family at the time. Like many others, my mother had lost everything during the war, so to find a silver object in the house was extremely unusual. I picked it up carefully and discovered my Christian name on it; my second name, though, was shown as "Heinrich." And then I turned it over and saw the writing on the other side. It read: "From your godfather, Heinrich Himmler."*

Guntram desperately wanted to ask his mother about the cup. But, as Gisela had been with me, she was secretive—and he knew how badly she would react to the revelation that he had been rummaging through her cupboards. It remained an unspoken and unsettling mystery.

In 1966 he first heard the word *Lebensborn*. His older sister needed her birth certificate in order to get married and was surprised to discover that she didn't have one. When she questioned their mother she was obstructive and told her daughter she didn't know where it was.

But an inquiry at her place of birth turned up the unexpected news that Guntram's sister was the illegitimate child of an army officer. Her records were still intact and showed that she had been born in a Lebensborn home. That led to the revelation that Guntram had also been a Lebensborn child. Rather than question his mother further, though, he chose to get away and moved to the United States. He stayed there for eight years and had a family of his own, putting aside the questions about his past.

But when his partner died in a car crash, he returned to Germany with his son; before long, the uncertainty about his roots began nagging at him again, and finally, in 1982, he decided to confront his mother during a long car journey where, as he put it, "she could not escape from me." He pulled off the road and forced his mother to talk to him.

*My mother was angry but she uttered three sentences that I will never forget: First she said: "I don't want to talk about that." Then she tried to stop me digging into my past: "People will throw dirt at you," she told me. Eventually, when she saw that I would not be put off, she made a promise to write the whole story down for me. I believed her and felt better, trusting that she would give me the truth.*

But she never did. For Guntram's mother, the truth was simply too difficult to speak about; she died two years later, taking her secrets to the grave and leaving Guntram both frustrated and angry. As she had once told him in an unguarded moment: "The relationship between mother and child is a power struggle." Guntram felt that he had been powerless in that struggle.

It wasn't until 2001, when he was fifty-eight, that Guntram discovered who his father was—not, as his mother had told him, a young soldier who died honorably, but an SS major-general who oversaw the deaths of tens of thousands of people while stationed in what is now western Poland. He had even been convicted of war crimes and sentenced to death by a Polish court in 1949, but had escaped to Argentina, where he died in 1970.

*My father was a war criminal. He was a man who allowed himself everything. And the SS enabled him to live that way. I assume my mother fell in love with a powerful military man.*

*He died peacefully and at his funeral his old comrades stood beside his grave and raised their right arms in the Nazi salute. I knew then that a racist is always a racist.*

There was a bitter irony to Guntram's description of his life. As a Lebensborn baby, his "racially pure" genes were supposed to have ensured that he grew up strong and confident—a future leader of the master race. Instead he had suffered for more than sixty years from feelings of low self-esteem, loneliness, and uncertainty. The only thing that helped, he told our meeting in Wernigerode, was finding other Lebensborn children.

*It has been a huge relief for me, although I haven't been able to shake this feeling of inadequacy. Maybe in ten years it will be gone. It's important that other children in Germany and abroad hear about this group because it could help.*

I agreed wholeheartedly with Guntram. I felt sure that Lebensspuren needed to be publicly discussed so that other men and women who had been through the Lebensborn program could make contact with us and perhaps find some solace. But in 2005 the group was not ready to do that; we were meeting privately—and one reason for that was the sense of shame that still attached to our past.

To some extent, Helga Kahrau exemplified the dilemma of all we faced, that of needing support and acceptance while simultaneously struggling with the painful reality of her birth. A tall and forceful woman, with her blond hair dyed a striking red, Helga had been born into the heart of the Nazi regime. During the war, her mother, Margarete, had been a secretary in the offices of Hitler's top aide, Martin Bormann, and of Joseph Goebbels. She had memories of growing up in privilege and comfort, surrounded by important-looking men in crisp uniforms.

In the decades that followed the end of the Third Reich, Margarete refused to talk to Helga about the war, much less tell her about the father she had never known. It was only after Margarete's death in 1993 that Helga began to examine her family's past. She was horrified by what she discovered.

Margarete was a fervent Nazi who barely knew Helga's father. He was a German army officer, and they met in June 1940 at a party celebrating Hitler's conquest of France. They had a one-night stand that left Margarete pregnant. She was a perfect candidate for Himmler's master race program: politically committed, racially pure, and expecting an illegitimate child from an equally Aryan German soldier. Nine months later Helga was born in the main Lebensborn home at Steinhöring, outside Munich.

When Helga was three months old, Margarete left the home and returned to work in Goebbels's Propaganda Ministry. Helga was handed over to foster parents; her new father was a high-ranking Nazi official in the occupied Polish city of Łodz. Here, Helga believed, he helped oversee the gassing of thousands of Jews at the nearby Chelmno concentration camp.

> *I spent the first four years of my life raised and tutored by the Nazi elite. I was involved, in a fundamental way, with murderers.*

At the end of the war Helga returned to Munich to be raised for the first time by her natural mother. Here she encountered the irony of Himmler's obsession with Nordic features. Although the city and its surrounding regions were the birthplace of Nazism, most Bavarians are dark-haired: the very racial characteristics that Lebensborn valued ensured that Helga stuck out.

> *I was big, blond, and Aryan, different from the southern Germans, and everyone asked me where I had come from. I couldn't answer them.*

The only document Helga possessed was a cryptic birth certificate from an "SS Mothers Home" that showed her mother's name but not that of her father. Nor was Margarete Kahrau willing to help her daughter understand. She deliberately concealed the truth, saying only that Helga's father had been a soldier who died in the war.

She was also reluctant to discuss what she had done in the service of Hitler's Reich; like most Germans of her generation, Margarete preferred to forget about the Nazis.

When Margarete died in 1993 Helga began investigating. She discovered Nazi files that provided detailed information about her foster father and the crimes he committed in the service of the Final Solution. But there was nothing in the documents about her biological father.

Then in 1994 she received a phone call. The man told her that he had been a Wehrmacht officer in Paris, that he had met Margarete for a single night of passion. He was now suffering from terminal cancer and wanted to reach out to his daughter. It was a bittersweet moment for Helga; she had found her real father at last, but only as he was dying. She decided to make the most of the time they had left and devoted herself to nursing him round the clock.

Her father had enjoyed a very successful postwar career in real estate, which had made him a multimillionaire. As his eldest child, Helga might have expected to inherit at least some of his estate. But when he died she encountered another legacy of her birth.

Her father left no will; shortly after his funeral Helga received a letter from his lawyers stating that because she was illegitimate, she could legally inherit nothing.

Since then, Helga had found some solace by visiting her birthplace, the Lebensborn home at Steinhöring. But she had never come to terms with her identity and worried constantly that people would assume she, like her mother and stepfather, was a Nazi.

*I grew up on the side of the murderers. Being a Lebensborn child is still a source of shame.*

Shame—the word that blighted the lives of so many of those who had been part of Himmler's plan to create a new master race. The more I heard from those who had been born into Lebensborn, rather than kidnapped to strengthen it, the more I felt proud to have been one of the *Banditenkinder*, the child of courageous partisans who fought against Nazi rule.

Gisela Heidenreich was four years old when she first encountered that shame: she overheard her uncle describe her as "an SS bastard." Gisela was sixty-three, a tall, strikingly Aryan-looking woman from Bavaria. She was a family therapist, a fact I noted with interest. There seemed to be a common trait in Lebensborn children; by accident or design, many of us had chosen careers in which we helped others overcome problems, while simultaneously struggling with our own.

Gisela described vividly the confusion she had suffered throughout her life and the web of lies that blighted her childhood. Her mother was Emilie Edelmann, the Lebensborn secretary who had given evidence at Nuremberg and who had been responsible for finding foster parents to take children stolen from the occupied countries.

Like so many of those who had been part of Lebensborn, Emilie was secretive and deceitful. At first she had led Gisela to believe that she was not her real mother but her aunt. Later she admitted that this was not true and that during the time she had worked in Himmler's bureaucracy she became pregnant following an affair with a married man. The SS packed her off to occupied Norway, to give birth in the Lebensborn home near Oslo. Several months later Emilie brought Gisela back to Germany.

Throughout her childhood Gisela's mother refused to answer any questions about the war. It was only after Emilie's death that Gisela discovered the depths of her mother's involvement with the Nazis.

She found a bundle of love letters between Emilie and Horst Wagner, the director of "Jewish Affairs" in the Reich's Foreign Office and its liaison with the SS. In this role, he aided in the roundup, deportation, and extermination of both German and foreign Jews.

Emilie's love affair with Wagner grew to the point where the couple considered formally making him Gisela's stepfather. Their relationship continued when the Reich fell and he was arrested by the Americans and held for trial at Nuremberg. But before he could be brought to justice he fled down one of the infamous "Ratlines" to South America.

Shocking though this was, it did not bring Gisela any closer to discovering the identity of her real father. It would be many years before she found out that he was the head of the SS officer school at Bad Toelz in Bavaria. She set out to track him down; when she did, her reaction both surprised her and helped her understand how so many Germans were able to live with knowledge of the crimes committed by the Nazis.

> *When I first met him it was on a station platform. I ran into his arms and all I thought was "I've got a father." In that instant I sanitized the person I knew my father was. And I never asked him what he did. My own reaction—that of an educated adult with knowledge of the Lebensborn program—has helped me to understand how people in those days just put the blinders on and ignored the terrible things that were happening.*

Gisela brought to our group a determination to rehabilitate the image of Lebensborn children. In part this was due to her experience of the postwar treatment of Norwegian babies born in the program's homes.

As I had heard at the first meeting in Hadamar, Norwegian hatred of the occupying German armies led to discrimination against the eight thousand children like Gisela born in its Lebensborn homes. At first the postwar government tried to have all the children shipped to Australia. When that plan failed—because Germany was in ruins, its population starving—some of the children were locked away in mental institutions or children's homes.

Gisela believed that this hatred and persecution was driven by Norway's national guilt at being occupied, the shame of its leaders having collaborated with the Nazis—and, above all, the wildly inaccurate rumors about Lebensborn homes as "SS stud farms." Three years earlier, the Norwegian government had quietly paid an average €24,000 compensation to the children it had victimized. Now, Gisela argued, the time had come to stop the lies and end the discrimination.

> *It's high time to tell the truth. There's been too much talk about Nazi babies, women being kept as SS whores, and tall blond people being bred. The Holocaust was about extinguishing so-called lesser races. Lebensborn was the reverse side of this coin: the idea was to further the Aryan race by whatever means were available.*
>
> *What I have learned is that I, and every other Lebensborn child, has a feeling of deep uncertainty about our identity; it is typical of us Lebensborn children. This has to stop.*

The stories of these "pure" Aryan children were harrowing. But theirs was only half the picture. There were others, like me, at the inaugural Lebensspuren meeting who had been forced, not born, into Himmler's program. Their accounts helped me understand how the process had worked.

What happened to Barbara Paciorkiewicz was typical. She was

born in 1938 in Gdynia, near Gdansk in Poland. Her family name then was Gajzler, but because her mother had died and her father had disappeared, she and her sister were separated, each one sent to live with one of their grandparents.

Gdansk was in the part of Poland under German occupation and the Nazis had renamed it Danzig. In 1942, when Barbara was four, the Youth Welfare Office issued instructions for all children to be brought to the regional youth welfare office in Łodz. Her grandmother took Barbara and was forced to leave her there.

There were a lot of children in the center. Each was measured—heads, chests, and hips—and weighed on scales. Then their faces were photographed from three angles. The people making these measurements were some of Himmler's race examiners; they were looking for racially suitable children to Germanize. Barbara had blond hair and looked Nordic. She was shipped off to a succession of different homes in Łodz.

*Here I was subjected to more tests—always there were more tests. Here we were forbidden—upon pain of punishment to speak Polish. Here every one of us was crying.*

Barbara's account of her kidnapping was similar to others I had heard. But her recollections of life in the Lebensborn home at Bad Polczyn provided me with new information about what my time in its care might have been like.

*This is where my memories truly begin. I can remember exactly where we were kept, the conditions there, and the treatment we received. There was a separation between us stolen children and those who had been born in the home.*

*All of us stolen children were kept on the ground floor of the building. The babies born in the home were kept on the floor above and we were never allowed to mix with them; nor were the staff who looked after these babies allowed to mix with the staff in charge of us. It was as if there was a hierarchy of our value: apparently the Nazis viewed the babies as more important than us children brought in for Germanization.*

*In the home we were constantly given medical tests—I think it must have been every day. We were in a big room on the ground floor which had a large semicircular wall of windows. I have been there since and this room still exists: it looks almost the same.*

*There was a very sinister atmosphere in the room and we were individually taken into a side room and given injections by a doctor. I fear now that these were to tranquilize us: I cannot see any other reason for it. And we children were terrified of these injections. All the children were crying in that room; no one ever laughed.*

Even for the precious Aryan babies like Guntram Weber, the regimen in Lebensborn homes was cold to the point of severity. They were separated from their mothers immediately after birth, and kept apart for the next twenty-four hours. Thereafter, they would be allowed only twenty minutes together every four hours; even during that brief period of contact the SS staff strongly discouraged mothers from caressing or talking to their children.

The older children were monitored constantly, and reports made about their behavior. Uncleanliness, bed-wetting, farting, nail-biting, and masturbation—which older boys were told on arrival was forbidden— were enough to ensure expulsion from the homes; these rejects were shipped off to forced education camps where they were brutalized and sometimes used as slave labor.

This Spartan regimen was intended to produce strong and ruthless future leaders for the master race. But children need love, not unyielding discipline. Barbara Paciorkiewicz remembered clearly how the rules frequently produced the opposite of the intended effect of Himmler's program.

*The children often reacted to them by wetting their beds. In the mornings when this was discovered, the children were beaten for this; even if only one had wet the bed, all of us were punished.*

Himmler's overall plan was the same for both types of Lebensborn children; for the duration of the war they were to be handed over to carefully vetted foster parents who would raise them as model Aryans.

After Germany's eventual victory the boys were to be sent to elite schools—the network of SS-run *Nationalpolitische Erziehungsanstalten*—where they would receive a strong physical and political education. The girls were to be sent to schools run by the Bund Deutscher Mädel—the female equivalent of the Hitler Youth—and trained to become housewives and mothers.

Barbara had also uncovered the way in which Lebensborn deliberately obscured the true identities of children stolen from the occupied territories.

First it erased all traces of where they had been plucked from, forbidding them to speak their own language; then it told would-be foster parents that the children were the orphans of fallen German soldiers. The men who ran the program—those who had been indicted and then acquitted at the Nuremberg trial—knew this to be a lie; but Himmler's orders made it clear that for youngsters like Barbara and me, every single trace of our previous life in Poland or Yugoslavia was to be erased.

Barbara's foster parents were from Lemgo in North Rhine–

Westphalia. The Rossmanns were in their fifties and had two grown-up sons who had been drafted into the Wehrmacht: they also had a daughter who had died of scarlet fever when she was nine. Neither was, as far as Barbara had been able to discover, a member of the Nazi Party: Herr Rossman was the director of a school and his wife was a housewife.

Although they were good and kind people who longed for a child to replace the daughter they had lost, even as a young child Barbara felt out of place in her new family. In particular, she suffered from nightmares in which unknown men came in through an open window to steal her.

*There was always an air of uneasiness at home. When I entered a room, everyone stopped talking. And I always asked myself: "What is it about me that makes this happen?"*

Back in Poland, Barbara's grandmother had never given up hope of finding her. At the end of the war she contacted the Red Cross; it located documents showing where Barbara was living. Very soon she was plucked from her foster family and placed in a temporary children's home run by the British Army. Six months later she was put on a train to Poland. She was eleven years old and had never been told about her biological parents, nor that she was anything other than a normal German child.

*I was very frightened and confused: I still thought the Rossmanns were my real parents and I didn't know anything about Poland. It didn't mean anything to me. I didn't speak Polish and I didn't even know I had a grandmother. It all seemed like a terrible journey into the unknown.*

I realized that I had never given any thought to what had happened to stolen children after the war. Perhaps because the von Oelhafens had kept me in the dark about my own circumstances, it had never occurred to me that other children had been traced and sent back to a country they could not remember. Barbara's story made me wonder whether—had I been given the choice—I would have wanted to be returned to Yugoslavia.

*The journey to Poland took a terribly long time. The train sometimes stood for days in a loop line. And then, suddenly, I heard people around me shout out "Poland Poland" and everyone was happy. I felt no joy when I arrived.*

*We were taken to a Red Cross camp at Katowice. It was chaos with people running around shouting out names. My grandmother had sent my uncle and he was shouting, but I had no idea who he was or what he was saying because he was speaking Polish. It was only when he shouted "Gajzler/Rossmann" that I realized. And I also realized at that moment that I had completely lost my identity.*

In the ruins of postwar Poland—a country with every reason to hate Germany—Barbara felt confused and isolated. Her uncle and his wife had been in a Nazi forced labor camp together with older children stolen from Gdynia but who were not deemed racially valuable.

Barbara was made to visit the former Stutthof concentration camp near Gdansk; her uncle forced her to look at the piles of children's shoes and the gas chambers: eighty-five thousand people had died here and he wanted her to see and understand what the Germans had done. But she still thought of herself as German. She found it impossible to believe what her uncle said.

*I thought German people were all good: that was how I had been brought up. It was even worse in school; the children played games in the playground in which Hitler was the bad guy. Because I was German, I was always picked as Hitler; but I didn't mind—in fact, in my ignorance I shouted out with pride that Hitler was my uncle.*

*I always thought that a terrible mistake had been made, that I had been mistaken for someone else, and this was why a good German girl like me was in this strange place.*

Barbara Paciorkiewicz spoke quietly and with dignity. But in her story I recognized the truth of our Lebensspuren motto. As Simone Weil had realized, all of us were still yearning to find and make a connection with our roots. Not being able to—because Lebensborn had destroyed our original identities and because our foster families often erected a wall of secrecy—had eaten away at the fabric of our lives for decades. Barbara spoke for all of us when she said how it had affected her, and how important our new organization could be.

*All my life I never felt good enough—nor did I know really who I was or where I was truly from. It hurts very much inside. I've always wanted to ask questions but until recently there was no one to ask.*

*Now I want to talk about this—even though it hurts—so the world does not forget the terrible idea of stealing children and racial tests. It must never happen again.*

The question was how to achieve this. There were only a few dozen of us at this first meeting—a fraction of the number of children born or kidnapped into Lebensborn—and already it was clear that there were differences between us. Some people felt we should step out of the shadows and hold a press conference; others wanted to concentrate on building a memorial here in Wernigerode, on the site of the old Lebensborn home. I sensed then that there would be difficulties and quarrels in the years ahead.

# SIXTEEN

# Taken

*At 6.30 am about 430 children aged between one and eighteen years were brought by cars to the railway track. The children had only such hand luggage as they could carry themselves. For breakfast they got black coffee and a small piece of bread.*

GERMAN RED CROSS MEMO,
*August 1942*

I N OCTOBER 2007 the final pieces of the puzzle fell into place.

    The previous two years had been busy. I was still working in my physiotherapy practice (though beginning to think about retiring), and Lebensspuren occupied much of my spare time. We went public in 2006; around forty Lebensborn children attended our second meeting in Wernigerode, along with journalists from the German and international press. Articles began appearing in quality newspapers and the BBC broadcast a story about what they called Hitler's Children around the world. Guntram Weber, Gisela Heidenreich, and I answered a never-ending stream of questions, convinced that openness was vital to educate the public about the truth of Himmler's master race experiment.

    The publicity seemed to work. Gradually it became possible to discuss Lebensborn, and the more it was talked about, the more inquiries Lebensspuren received from people who suspected they might have been part of it. The following year more than sixty people came to the meeting in Wernigerode.

It would be pleasant—though probably naive—to believe that it was our frankness that helped open the archives whose personnel had always proved so resistant to giving out information. But for whatever reason, previously unhelpful organizations finally began to open their files. The most important was the International Tracing Service in Bad Arolsen.

The ITS had long been criticized for refusing fully to open up its millions of files. It had claimed, with the backing of the German government, that the federal law required a hundred years to pass from the creation of records to their public release. It was an odd argument: because of its multinational funding and oversight arrangements, ITS was not technically subject to German law. Its critics alleged that a desire to suppress information about the Holocaust in Germany was the real reason for its secrecy.

The fact that in January 2000 all eleven governments sitting on the International Commission of the ITS had endorsed a call for the opening of Nazi archives worldwide seemed to support this view. In March 2006 the U.S. Holocaust Memorial Museum publicly accused the International Tracing Service and the International Committee of the Red Cross of obstruction.

*The ITS and the ICRC have consistently refused to cooperate . . .*
*and have kept the archive closed.*

Two months later the ITS announced that it would finally open its archives in the autumn of 2007.

For seven years I had waited to see the documents the organization held about me and my family. Two requests had produced only an acknowledgment that there were relevant files, but that time was needed "to evaluate" them, followed by a letter in 2003 asking me for any information I had discovered myself.

When they eventually arrived, the documents told me a great deal about both my biological family and Gisela von Oelhafen. The first was a set of papers detailing what had happened to Johann Matko; they showed the dates he had been arrested for partisan activity and held in Mauthausen concentration camp. With typical efficiency the Nazis had recorded his name on the lists of political prisoners. I could not help but wonder at why the International Tracing Service had withheld these papers from me for so long.

The second tranche of documents came from Lebensborn files; these showed that Ingrid von Oelhafen was once known as Erika Matko from St. Sauerbrunn in Yugoslavia. They even included a copy of an insurance policy that Lebensborn had taken out in my name. Again, I could not understand why I had not been given these papers before. I had wasted valuable time trying to locate St. Sauerbrunn in Austria; yet all along, the ITS had clear evidence that showed I came from Yugoslavia.

But it was the third bundle of records that really shocked me. It was a series of letters from various branches of the Red Cross dating back to the immediate postwar years.

These showed that in 1949 two separate agencies had been searching for me, with a view to returning me to my real family. The first was Caritas, the international Catholic relief organization that had been tasked with overseeing the work of all welfare organizations accredited to the United Nations. Caritas officials had been on the trail of children stolen from Nazi-occupied countries—and in particular from Yugoslavia—and must have found my name on the list of transports. They had written to the Yugoslavian Red Cross asking for help in locating me.

At the same time the international branch of the Red Cross—which then had overall responsibility for tracking down and repatriating displaced persons—was also searching for me. It, too, had written to the Yugoslavian Red Cross in an attempt to confirm my true identity.

Surprisingly, given the difficulties caused by the Cold War and by the need to create a new, unified country, Yugoslavian officials responded. They did not have much in the way of documents themselves—most Nazi files had been destroyed in the fighting or in desperate last-minute bonfires—but they were able to issue an urgent request to the International Tracing Service office in Hamburg. It asked for social workers from the German branch of the Red Cross to visit the von Oelhafen family in Hamburg to ascertain whether I was living with them and whether I was Erika Matko.

I thought back and quickly realized that in 1949 I was not in Hamburg, but in the children's home at Langeoog to which Gisela had sent me the day after we escaped to the west. Unless my foster parents chose to help them, the officials would have had no chance of finding and interviewing me.

The final document showed that Gisela, at least, was not terribly forthcoming.

*GERMAN RED CROSS,*
*Central Zone, Hamburg*
*25 October, 1950*

*To: The International Tracing Service Child Search Branch, Arolsen*
*Subject: MATKO, Erika, born on 11/11/1941 in St. Sauerbrunn*

*The wife of von Oelhafen was visited by us. We could not get information from the husband because he does not currently live in Hamburg.*

*Frau von Oelhafen has been away on a trip for some time. However, she picked up in person the child identified above from the children's home Kohren-Sahlis at Leipzig and therefore should be able to provide the best information.*

*However, the only thing she has on paper is a vaccination certificate from Kohren-Sahlis, of which we enclose a copy. Frau von Oelhafen drove to Kohren-Sahlis at the instigation of the Lebensborn Society in Munich. There she was told that Erika Matko was an ethnic German child.*

*At that point the child Dietmar Holzapfel had already been living with the von Oelhafens for half a year: he had been picked up from the Municipal baby nursing home at Munich. The father of this child is missing at Stalingrad.*

*Erika MATKO will continue to remain as a foster child with Frau von Oelhafen. An adoption of the child is not intended. Frau von Oelhafen is always happy to make additional information available. She also has a self-interest in learning about the origin of the child, so that she can answer the child's questions. However, she cannot contribute to any further details, having no documents about the child.*

*The von Oelhafens also fled from the Russians, and in doing so lost their belongings. Frau von Oelhafen remembers that she probably received a transfer note [for Erika Matko] from the children's home at Kohren-Sahlis. This was lost while she was on the run.*

*We regret that we can currently give you no further information. We would be very grateful if you would inform us of the outcome of your negotiations in St. Sauerbrunn.*

Without Gisela's cooperation—and because Lebensborn had destroyed all records of my true identity—there was no hope of finding my biological parents, much less returning me to them. All the organizations involved abandoned their efforts at this point.

I was astonished. Gisela had never once told me that she had been contacted by the Red Cross—not even during the years when I was struggling to obtain official documents from the German government. Nor had she ever even hinted that she knew my original identity. But worst of all, I knew she had misled the social workers; she had told them that the "transfer note," given to her and Hermann when I was handed over to their care by Lebensborn, had been lost when we escaped from the Russian sector in 1947. Yet I had found that same document when I cleared out her room in the 1990s.

I find it hard, even now, to speak badly of Gisela. Deep down I still want her to love me, even though she is long gone. But I have to put aside these emotions. I must recognize this for what it was: a betrayal. She knowingly hid the truth from me. I was glad—happy, even—to know that someone had been looking for me all those years ago, but I was very hurt to know how the search had been obstructed by the woman I had once called my mother.

That same month I made my second visit to Slovenia. I organized my trip to coincide with the annual meeting of stolen children in Celje, and I arranged to travel on from there to Rogaška Slatina, where I was to meet up again with Maria Matko and her family. But I was also being filmed for a German television program; the reporter had arranged for me to spend a day with local historians in Maribor.

I don't know whether it was the presence of the cameras or simply that the Slovenian authorities had managed to unearth more evidence, but my welcome there was warmer than it had been two years earlier, and the meeting much more productive. I learned at last exactly what happened in Celje—and the truth about Erika Matko.

The occupation of Yugoslavia in the spring of 1941 began well for Germany. Its troops advanced swiftly through the country and in just ten days the Yugoslav High Command capitulated.

On April 16, the day of surrender, the Gestapo moved into Celje and began to arrest local anti-Nazi partisans. Three days later Himmler himself arrived to inspect the town's ancient prison, Stari Pisker. In the coming months it would be used for the torture and execution of hundreds of resistance fighters.

But unlike other countries overrun by the German Blitzkrieg, Yugoslavia was never fully conquered. Resistance was organized by the charismatic Josip Tito. On July 4, 1941, he issued a secretly printed call to rise up against the Nazi occupiers.

*Peoples of Yugoslavia: Serbs, Croats, Slovenes, Montenegrins, Macedonians and others! Now is the time, the hour has struck to rise like one man, in the battle against the invaders and hirelings, killers of our peoples. Do not falter in the face of any enemy terror. Answer terror with savage blows at the most vital points of the Fascist occupation bandits. Destroy everything—everything that is of use to the Fascist invaders. Do not let our railways carry equipment and other things that serve the Fascist hordes . . . Workers, Peasants, Citizens, and Youth of Yugoslavia . . . battle against the Fascist occupation hordes who are striving to dominate the whole world.*

This led to an intensive guerrilla campaign against the Germans. By September 1941 there were at least seventy thousand resistance fighters active in Yugoslavia. Tito's partisans engaged in classic hit-and-run tactics, and when the Germans launched a major counteroffensive against the rebels, they simply retreated into the mountains. Hitler's response to this (as well as to partisan activity across all the occupied countries) was the *Nacht und Nebel* decree. Literally translated, this meant "night and fog"; in practice, it was an order to murder anyone who dared oppose Nazi rule. On December 7 the instructions were sent out to commanders in the field.

*Within the occupied territories, communistic elements and other circles hostile to Germany have increased their efforts against the German State and the occupying powers . . .*

*The amount and the danger of these machinations oblige us to take severe measures as a deterrent. First of all the following directives are to be applied:*

*1. Within the occupied territories, the adequate punishment for offences committed against the German State or the occupying power which endanger their security or a state of readiness is, on principle, the death penalty.*

*2. The offences listed in paragraph I as a rule are to be dealt with in the occupied countries only if it is probable that sentence of death will be passed upon the offender, or at least the principal offender, and if the trial and the execution can be completed in a very short time. Otherwise the offenders, at least the principal offenders, are to be taken to Germany.*

*3. Prisoners taken to Germany are subject to military procedure only if particular military interests require this. In case German or foreign authorities enquire about such prisoners, they are to be told that they have been arrested but that the proceedings do not allow any further information.*

*4. The Commanders in the occupied territories and the Court*
*authorities within the framework of their jurisdiction are*
*personally responsible for the observance of this decree.*

The same day, Himmler issued instructions to his Gestapo and SS
forces.

*After lengthy consideration, it is the will of the Führer that the*
*measures taken against those who are guilty of offences against the*
*Reich or against the occupation forces in occupied areas should be*
*altered. The Führer is of the opinion that in such cases penal servi-*
*tude or even a hard labour sentence for life will be regarded as a*
*sign of weakness.*

*An effective and lasting deterrent can be achieved only by the*
*death penalty or by taking measures which will leave the family*
*and the population uncertain as to the fate of the offender. Depor-*
*tation to Germany serves this purpose.*

It was a deliberate rejection of the laws of war. No longer would
the Geneva Conventions or any other regulations protect the civilian
population of occupied territories. On December 12, Feldmarschall
Wilhelm Keitel, chief of the German Supreme High Command,
issued his own reinforcement of Hitler's decree to Wehrmacht troops
throughout the expanded German Reich.

*Efficient and enduring intimidation can only be achieved either*
*by capital punishment or by measures by which the relatives of the*
*criminals do not know the fate of the criminal.*

*In order to nip disorders in the bud the sternest measures must*
*be applied at the first sign of insurrection. It should also be taken*

*into consideration that in the countries in question a human life is often valueless. In a reprisal for the life of a German soldier, the general rule should be capital punishment for 50–100 Communists. The manner of execution must have a frightening effect.*

But the campaign failed to terrorize the population into submission. Tito's partisan army grew in numbers and in effectiveness. By the middle of 1942, Himmler issued orders for an even greater crackdown on resistance. On June 25 he put Obergruppenführer Erwin Rösener, head of SS forces in the region, in charge of anti-Resistance operations and ordered him to murder or imprison all families suspected of involvement with the rebels.

Rösener carefully planned six separate *Aktionen*, or campaigns, in the Lower Styria area, centered on Maribor. In the first of these, on July 22, 1942, one thousand people—men, women, and children—were arrested and brought to Celje. The men were separated from their families and one hundred were lined up against the walls of Stari Pisker, then summarily executed by firing squad. The killings were photographed by Nazi cameramen as a warning against partisan activity.

The images were processed at a local photographer's studio; he made extra copies in secret and hid them until the end of the war. It was sobering to hold these pictures in my hands. Among the murdered men that day was Ignaz Matko. Was he one of the bodies lying against the courtyard wall, or being lifted onto a stretcher by those who would be shot next?

Some of the other adults snatched in the roundup were held as hostages, to ensure the compliance of the surrounding towns and villages with future *Aktionen*.

The remainder, both men and women, were shipped to concentration camps like Auschwitz. Here, they were murdered or worked and starved to death. Their children were transported to Frohnleiten, in Austria, for racial examinations. Those deemed suitably Aryan— there were not many—were taken away for Germanization; the rest were sent to "education camps," where they were treated brutally and suffered from hunger and disease.

The second *Aktion* was scheduled for the beginning of the following month. Orders were issued that all families in the nearby villages were to report to the school at Celje on August 3.

Johann and Helena Matko were among the hundreds of families who arrived at the school yard that morning with their three children, Tanja, Ludvig, and Erika. They were met by heavily armed soldiers who quickly separated them into three groups, one for the men and one for women; the children were pulled from them and taken inside.

Once again, a photographer recorded the event. One picture shows families lined up against the outside wall; a second captured the moment when the troops separated them. In this frame a woman in a head scarf is being restrained by a Wehrmacht officer, while a second soldier, his rifle slung from his shoulder, stands in front of a mother carrying a baby; she appears to be pleading with him.

A third photograph was shot inside the school. In a crude wooden structure, lined with straw, children and babies are being undressed by unidentified helpers. One little boy appears to be struggling; the faces of others, though, are blank and emotionless.

Looking at these pictures, I felt two quite separate emotions. Both stemmed from the realization that somewhere in the crowd in the yard or among the babies in the schoolroom was Erika Matko; these grainy black-and-white photographs recorded the day I was stolen from my family.

My first reaction was fear. I do not wish to sound melodramatic, but I felt a shiver run through my body, an uncontrollable trembling and a sensation of utter loneliness and vulnerability. But there was anger, too. How could anyone treat children like this? What could these soldiers have been thinking when they snatched babies from their mothers and imprisoned them in what amounted to a cattle pen?

Throughout my life I have tried to hide my emotions, to bury them so deeply that the feelings of loss, abandonment, and powerlessness could not rise up to engulf me. These photographs stripped away that protective layer. I was Erika once again.

The other children and I were kept in the schoolroom for two days. We were crudely assessed for racial value. Blond hair, light-colored skin, and blue eyes were taken as a sign of Aryan blood; brown hair and dark skin or eyes were the marks of worthless Slavonic ancestry. I was designated valuable, while Tanja and Ludvig were rejected. They were sent outside and handed back to our parents.

In total, 430 youngsters were judged to be Aryan. We were held in the schoolroom and then taken to the train station. The older children carried babies like me in baskets. The German Red Cross (DRK) was on hand to supervise this children's transport. The leadership of this organization were committed Nazis—even to the point of wearing uniforms and ceremonial daggers—but below them was a civilian army of volunteers. I was handed a report by one of these workers, a woman named Anna Rath.

*At 6.30 am about 430 children aged between one and eighteen years were brought by cars to the railway track. The children had only such hand luggage as they could carry themselves. For break-fast they got black coffee and a small piece of bread.*

*The embarkation went smoothly. At 10.30 am a delay of one hour was announced. The train started but only travelled until*

*2.45 pm. The children then had to endure a four hour wait: during this time neither the Red Cross nor officials from the National Socialist People's Welfare Organization provided any food for them. Fresh water was only brought by a DRK helper who accompanied the train.*

*Once they arrived in Frohnleiten, the DRK helpers and the young children (two to five years of age) had to walk to the resettlement camp, carrying suitcases and bundles. The children were half-naked and hungry, some with very dirty nappies: this was because there were no clothes to change them. They were screaming and crying.*

*When we arrived [at the camp] there was another delay for the children because no food was ready for them. They had to stay outside in the courtyard and in a meadow. Finally, at 5 pm the children were allowed to go into the eating room. The 16 DRK accompanying assistants, although tired and weary themselves (they had been on duty since 4.30 am) had to look after the children because all the camp staff, save for four people, were on vacation.*

This was how the Nazis treated the "racially valuable" children they stole. This was how my life in their hands began. No wonder, then, that I have struggled all my life with a longing to be loved.

In Frohnleiten there were more tests. Himmler's race examiners prodded and poked us, measuring and recording our every characteristic before assigning us to one of four categories. The top two ensured a place in a Lebensborn home; the others guaranteed a ticket to a re-education camp. Among those assessing the kidnapped Yugoslavian children was Inge Viermetz, the female official who had been tried but acquitted at Nuremberg; she was operating on written instructions to "take only young children who have not yet reached school age."

But it appeared that Lebensborn was not the only organization that wanted us. Officials from VoMi, the agency Himmler had set up to "protect" ethnic Germans living outsider the old Reich, wanted their share of the racially valuable children who would become the future leaders of the master race. According to testimony given at Nuremberg, *"a real competition for these children arose between VoMi and Lebensborn, and it was thanks to Frau Viermetz's efforts that Lebensborn won in the end."*

I LOOKED AT this evidence and marveled again at the decision of the judges at Nuremberg to acquit Viermetz and the other senior Lebensborn officials. She had quite literally handled stolen goods; she had decided the fates of hundreds of children—from all over the occupied countries—sending some of them into a program that erased their identities, and the rest to camps where many died. How could this woman have been declared innocent?

I was moved from Frohnleiten to another camp, at Werdenfels, near Regensburg in Bavaria. At the end of 1942, Lebensborn sent Emilie Edelmann—Gisela Heidenreich's mother—to supervise further racial selection tests. She must have decided that I was good enough; the forms were signed and I was shipped off to Kohren-Sahlis.

Ours was not the last transport of Yugoslavian children. The documents I was shown in Maribor revealed that there had been four further *Aktionen* in which hundreds more families were summoned to Celje for racial examination, sifting, and separation. They, too, were divided up between Lebensborn homes and reeducation camps.

THE OFFICIALS WHO showed me these papers had one more revelation. It turned out to be both a mystery and a clue as to why there were two Erika Matkos.

Johann and Helena had arrived at the school yard with three children. When they were permitted to leave, the records showed that they went home with three children—Tanja and Ludvig and a baby girl called Erika. I knew that my sister and brother had been handed back to my parents, but who was this other child? How could Erika Matko have been simultaneously on the train to Frohnleiten and on the journey back to Rogaška Slatina with Johann and Helena? It made no sense, yet it had definitely happened.

It was Maria Matko who led me toward the answer. We met in her house the day after my visit to Maribor. After the initial shock of the DNA results, she had accepted that I was her sister-in-law. Now, with her help, I was finally able to piece together what had happened to me.

On the day that the children were handed back to Johann and Helena, the Nazis executed several suspected partisans in Celje prison. Witnesses recalled that the families waiting outside the school yard heard the volleys of shots. The children of those murdered men and women were being held with me inside the schoolroom; some were now orphans.

When Tanja and Ludvig were returned to her, Helena must have complained that her third child was missing. Perhaps to appease her or because they did not know what to do with it, the Germans handed her an orphaned baby. This was the girl who grew up as Erika Matko.

I was torn between pain, anger, and bewilderment. I knew that my mother must have realized that the baby thrust into her arms was not her own. It wouldn't have looked the same, nor would it have smelled right, in that indefinable way that mothers know the smell of their own baby. So how could she have accepted this cynical substitution?

The only explanation I could imagine was that she was too terrified to argue; that the sound of the firing squads made her fearful for her own life and those of her husband and children. But rational understanding was one thing, emotion quite another. For almost sixty years I had been deeply troubled by not knowing who I really was; for the past seven years I had been on a long and harrowing journey to unravel the mystery of my past and discover how I had been transformed from Erika Matko to Ingrid von Oelhafen.

Now I knew. And it didn't help at all.

SEVENTEEN

## Searching

*What are we doing? I asked myself. What in God's name are we doing?*

GITTA SERENY,
FORMER UNRRA CHILD WELFARE OFFICER

ALL THE RESENTMENT and hurt that I had suppressed throughout my life now surfaced.

I was angry with everyone involved in my story. Angry with Hitler and Himmler for the orders to kidnap me and deny me the love of my own family; angry with Inge Viermetz and the Lebensborn officials for concealing my true identity and reinventing me as a German child. I hated what these Nazis had done to me and to all the other victims of their obsession with pure blood and the Aryan master race.

But my rage was also focused on those much closer to me. Gisela and Hermann von Oelhafen had been willing accomplices in this wretched scheme. They surely should have realized that Lebensborn was not to be trusted. Even in wartime Germany there had been enough information—and, indeed rumor—about the organization for them to have had doubts about the provenance of a baby it was offering for fostering.

And then there was Gisela's strange ambivalence toward me; sending me to the foster homes hardly suggested someone who was committed to bringing up a child in a warm and loving environment. Worse, her evasiveness and deceptions about my origins had hampered my search for the truth. How much easier would my life had been if she had told me where I came from? I knew from my friends in Lebensspuren that some women who fostered Lebensborn children had been open and honest, and that this had eased some of the children's anxieties. Why did Gisela choose not to talk to me?

But it was the actions of my biological family that hurt the most. I could not bring myself to condemn Helena and Johann Matko for accepting the baby handed to them by the Nazis. I realized that a family of known partisans could not—especially on a day when their compatriots were being executed—have complained. I put myself in their place and tried to imagine the fear of a knock on the door and the discovery of a Gestapo or SS officer standing outside. Although I was haunted by the thought that this other Erika grew up to live what should have been my life, safe in the warmth of a mother's love rather than deposited like a parcel in children's homes or left with a sick and frightening foster father, I understood how it had happened and could forgive.

WHAT I COULD not accept was that Helena had continued with the lie long after the end of the war. Why had she never once tried to find me? Barbara Paciorkiewicz's story had shown me that some families of kidnapped children had been determined to bring home their stolen youngsters. How could Helena have lived with the knowledge that her real baby was somewhere in Germany? How could she have kept on going without once trying to find me?

I would have loved to ask her that question. But Helena died in 1994; at that time I had not even found the documents Gisela had hidden from me, much less discovered that my roots lay in Slovenia. The actions of my real and my foster mother had conspired to rob me of the chance to seek answers.

My emotions needed a scapegoat: someone living who I could blame for my position. Erika Matko—the other Erika—became the focus of all my anger and pain. Her refusal to meet me, even to answer my letter, enraged me. I could not understand how anyone could be so callous. The thought that she had stolen my life gnawed away inside of me. Maria had told me that the other Erika had been ill much of her life and as a result had never worked. That, presumably, was the benefit of growing up behind the Iron Curtain; people may not have had the freedom Gisela sought for us by escaping to the west, but they did have the security of a state welfare system.

I THOUGHT HOW hard I had worked to build my physiotherapy business and the difficulties I had encountered with German bureaucracy, and compared this to the way Erika had apparently been supported by her government. And my anger grew.

My friends tried to reason with me. It was not, they rightly pointed out, Erika's fault that she had been given my identity. As a child, she could not have known how our lives were swapped, and nor could she have done anything about it.

And after the war; in Tito's Yugoslavia would it have been possible for Helena and Johann to reveal any brush they'd had with the German occupiers? Probably not; the Communists were not always scrupulous about the innocence or otherwise of those tainted by any form of involvement with the Nazis. Most likely Erika never knew the truth about her origins; perhaps no one except my parents knew.

Other people urged me to imagine what it must have been like for Erika when I first contacted her. She was then over sixty and suffering from a severe heart condition; it must have been an enormous shock for a complete stranger suddenly to appear and challenge everything she knew about identity. It must have felt terribly menacing. Could I not sympathize?

I could not. I was too consumed by the injustice of everything that had happened to allow myself to feel sorry for a woman whose life I had surely turned upside down.

It took a long while for the anger to dissipate. As months, and then years, passed, I gradually became able to analyze the situation more clearly. I began to examine what an alternate history would have looked like for me. I thought again of Barbara's story of being taken away from her German foster family and the only home she could really remember; I made myself imagine myself on the train with her to Poland and tried to feel her bewilderment.

I knew from meeting the group of stolen children in Celje that some of those kidnapped from Yugoslavia had been returned to their families. There had even been a court case to set a precedent for these repatriations. Ivan Petrochik had been snatched by an SS detachment in 1943 when he was less than two years old. His father had been shot by the Gestapo and his mother sent to a concentration camp. He was given the label *Banditenkind* and handed by Lebensborn to a Germany family. His mother survived the war and searched for seven years to trace him. In 1952 a court ordered Ivan to be returned to Yugoslavia; he was eleven years old and had been raised for most of that time as a German child.

The stories of Ivan and Barbara forced me to wonder how the process of repatriation worked and what effect it had on everyone involved. In 2014 I found some of the answers.

Gitta Sereny was then a highly respected journalist and author. She had been born in Vienna in 1921, the daughter of an Austrian aristocrat and a former actress from Hamburg.

When she was thirteen her parents sent her away to boarding school in England; but her train was delayed in Nuremberg and she witnessed one of the Nazis' mass rallies. It left an indelible mark on her, and when she finished school she moved to France to help orphans suffering under the German occupation. She also worked with the French resistance.

When the war ended she joined the United Nations Relief and Rehabilitation Administration—UNRRA—working to repatriate the millions of displaced people scattered across the former Reich. But soon she was assigned to the Child Tracing Department; fifty-three years later she published an account of her experiences in a now-defunct magazine.* In it she described the repatriation of a young boy and girl from Germany to Poland, and for the first time I truly understood what being returned to Yugoslavia would have meant for me.

The process began with Sereny visiting the foster home. It was a traditional Bavarian single-story farmhouse, its windows uncurtained and with only two dim lights showing the way to the front door. Sereny had prepared for the visit by examining the region's population records in the local mayor's office. Six people were registered as living at the farm: the farmer and his wife, both in their midforties, and his elderly parents. There were also two young children—a boy and a girl.

She was keenly aware of the potential distress her visit, and the uncomfortable questions she needed to ask, would cause. It was vital

---

* *Talk* magazine. Reproduced in the Jewish Virtual Library, 2009. The magazine ceased publication several years ago and Gitta Sereny died in 2012.

to see the children in the family surroundings, but she hoped that before the interview went too far, the youngsters would be sent to bed.

Her reception was distinctly chilly. The family sat around the kitchen table and deliberately declined to stand up when Sereny stepped inside. Although the farmer, his wife, and the two children shook her proffered hand—the boy uneasily, the girl enthusiastically—the grandfather refused to do so, hiding his hand behind his back and gruffly demanding what this intruder wanted.

THE CHILDREN WERE called Johann and Marie. Both were officially six years old and both had blue eyes and blond hair—the boy's cut short and crudely, the girl's longer and neatly braided. Sereny explained that she only wanted to talk with the family for a short time. To ease the frosty atmosphere she gave each of the children a chocolate bar—a precious gift in the austerity of postwar Germany. It provoked, though, a mixed reaction.

> *It was when the little girl, beaming, said, "Danke," and I stroked her face, that the farmer's wife said sharply, "Geht zu Bett"* [Go to bed], *and the two children shot up to obey.*

The little girl hugged her mother and reached out for her father's hand. The little boy politely, but formally, bade his parents good night then gave Sereny a suspicious look before kissing his grandfather. Then the farmer took the two children away and put them to bed, holding them tightly as he did so.

In 1945 there were 8,500 "unaccompanied children of United Nations and assimilated nationality" registered in the tracing service's files. Within months, tens of thousands of new names were added, sometimes accompanied by snapshots or physical descriptions, all of the names belonging to children kidnapped from the east for Himmler's Germanization program. Marie and Johann were among them. Gitta expressed her disbelief at this situation:

*Who would have taken babies or toddlers away from mothers? . . . How could anyone, even bigots gone mad, believe they could discern "racial values" in young, undeveloped children? Above all how, in practice, could there now be large numbers of foreign children—at least some of whom would have to be old enough to have memories—living, basically in hiding, within the German community?*

The farmer was hostile when Sereny began asking questions. He said that their son had been killed by the Red Army during the siege of Stalingrad; his sister had died four years earlier in a road accident. They had fostered Johann and Marie to replace their lost children. It was plain that this family loved the children, and Sereny tried to reassure the farmers that she understood this while simultaneously insisting that they must disclose everything they knew about the youngsters' origins.

When she asked about their biological parents, the farmer's wife said that they had died, but was very vague about who had given her this information. Sereny pushed harder, explaining to the family that many Eastern European parents were searching for children who had been stolen from them.

*"East?" said the grandfather and, repeating it, virtually spat out the hated word: "East? Our children have nothing to do with 'east.'*

*They are German, German orphans. You need only look at them."*
*And there it was: "You need only look at them."*

Somebody had indeed once looked at them. Just as had happened in Celje, villagers around the city of Łodz had been instructed to bring their children to the Youth Welfare Office, where the race examiners had done their work and shipped the chosen children off to Lebensborn. Johann and Marie's parents had been searching for them ever since and had photographs to support their claim. UNRRA decided the children were to be returned to them.

Gitta Sereny was deployed away from the area shortly afterward. Then, in the summer of 1946, she was sent to work in a children's center in Bavaria. To her surprise—and dismay—she found that Johann and Marie were being held there. They were plainly struggling to cope with their removal from the farmer and his wife; both had deep shadows under their eyes and their skin was unhealthily pale. Sereny was shocked by their condition.

*Marie was scrunched up in a chair, her eyes closed, the lids trans-*
*parent, her thumb in her mouth, but Johann raced up as soon as*
*he saw me, and shouting hoarsely, "Du! Du! Du!" ["You! You!*
*You!"], hit out at me with feet and fists . . .*

The staff at the center had seen all of this before; the children's pitiful state was, they told Sereny, all too typical of other youngsters who had been taken away from their German foster families prior to being sent back to their countries of birth. Many, including Johann and Marie, had to be kept in the unit after their official repatriation date; it seemed the only way to ease the pain of what was, after all, the second separation in their young lives and to prepare them for the overpowering expectations of their biological parents. Experience showed that these reunions placed a terrible mental strain on already traumatized children.

This was a caring and thoughtful approach—but for Johann and Marie it had clearly failed. The young boy was already showing signs of aggression, while his sister had effectively reverted to babyhood; she wet the bed frequently and would only eat when fed from a bottle.

Later that night, the resident psychiatrist suggested that Sereny try feeding Marie with a bottle.

*She lay there, her eyes shut, the only movement in her lips, which sucked, and in her small throat, which swallowed. I held her until she was asleep. It helped me but, I fear, not her.*

*What are we doing? I asked myself. What in God's name are we doing?*

Now I understood. This would have been my fate, had I been sent back to Rogaška Slatina. I cannot believe that I would have understood what was happening, any more than Johann and Marie grasped why they were taken from the only family they could remember. And now, at last, I was angry no more.

# EIGHTEEN

## Peace

*My identity might begin with the fact of my race but it didn't, couldn't, end there.*

BARACK OBAMA,

*DREAMS FROM MY FATHER:*

*A STORY OF RACE AND INHERITANCE, 1995*

W HAT IS IDENTITY? How is it formed? And does identity shape the person—or is it the other way around?

This is not, as it might seem, merely an exercise in abstract philosophy. As my journey ended it was the question that I had to face up to. I knew now who I was—or had once been. What I was less sure about was what this meant.

Identity is much more than just the answer to the question "Who are we?" It is also about personality. But how had I become Ingrid von Oelhafen? Was I the product of the first years of my life as a Lebensborn child? Was it that which dictated who I became thereafter? Was it to blame for my shyness, my lack of confidence, and my desire to put the needs of others—of children especially—above my own? In other words, was the course of my life set in stone by Himmler? That, after all, was what he intended; all of us born or kidnapped into Lebensborn were supposed to fulfill his vision of a new and uniform generation of the German master race.

Surely I was just as much the product of my own choices? Genetics might dictate hair and skin color, but identity must involve an element of free will. I had chosen to devote my life to handicapped children, chosen not to get married and have a family of my own. These were my decisions—not the ineluctable result of the Lebensborn program.

Perhaps those who have never endured the uncertainty of not knowing their identity are rarely troubled by these existential questions. And yet which of us doesn't, in our darker moments, return again and again to a particular moment of our lives and wonder what would have happened had events played out differently?

In Shakespeare's *Hamlet*, Ophelia says, *"We know what we are, but not what we may be."* I could not help but dwell on what might have been. What if I had failed the racial examination that day in Celje? What would my life have been, growing up as Erika Matko? Would I have had the opportunity to have a rewarding career, or would my horizons have been limited—as seemed to have been the case with the other Erika—by my environment? If Gisela had been more honest and if the Cold War had not intervened, I would have been reunited with my biological parents. What would that have meant for the course of my life? I asked myself whether I would have been better off had the Nazis left me with my family, or whether, in some twisted irony, they did me what turned out to be a favor?

The annual meetings of Lebensborn children exacerbated this uncertainty. The tensions that I had detected at our first gathering had grown steadily over the years until Lebensspuren was riven by arguments. All of us had been damaged by our involvement in the master race experiment; all of us struggled to come to terms with our personal histories. By 2014 many of those who had joined together to create a supportive environment had walked out or drifted away to form new and smaller groups. I was one of them.

But that year I made two trips that helped me find some peace. The first was a visit to a former Lebensborn employee, Anneliese Beck. Now ninety-two and almost blind, when I arrived at her home near Frankfurt, she greeted me with tea and Stollen cake.

Frau Beck had worked at the Sonnenwiese home in Kohren-Sahlis at the time when I was kept there. She did not remember me; there were 150 youngsters living there, and I had not been in the group for which she was responsible. But she was able to tell me a great deal about the daily routine at Sonnenwiese and to help me understand what my life would have been like on its premises. She showed me a photograph of herself with some of the children. I was pleased to see that they were very well dressed and clearly well fed. And she was adamant in insisting that despite the circumstances and the presence of the SS, for the most part our time in Kohren-Sahlis was happy and comfortable.

Sitting with Frau Beck helped me fill one of the last remaining gaps in my knowledge. I had no memories of Sonnenwiese, and though I often tried, I was unable to visualize the years I spent there; no matter how much I forced myself to think about it, all I could see was a dark hole. Now that hole was filled and the walls that protected me from my memories were beginning to crumble. I sensed that the final stage would be to travel to Kohren-Sahlis, to walk inside the buildings there; doing this would, I felt sure, unlock my mind. I was not yet strong enough to go—but I knew that in the coming years I would make that journey.

In October 2014 I returned to Slovenia. I went first to Rogaška Slatina and, in a pretty public park, paid my respects at the memorial to the men and women who were shot between 1941 and 1945. More than one hundred names were carved into the stone. I looked for my uncle Ignaz's, and when I found it, I traced the letters with my fingertips.

Later, Maria Matko showed me the house where I was born before taking me to a cemetery sitting on the top of a hill, where my parents, my grandmother, my brother, and my sister are all buried. I laid flowers on the graves and lit candles for my sister and brother while Maria and her niece cleaned the paths around the stones. I had expected to be overwhelmed by a sense of loss, and so I was surprised to discover that aside from the normal sadness of visiting a graveyard, I felt very little.

It was a similar story later in the afternoon when Maria invited me back to her apartment for Slovenian coffee and homemade blueberry liqueur with other members of the family. The atmosphere was warm and friendly; everyone was hospitable and open. The Matkos had clearly come to accept me as one of their own, and they gave me photographs of my parents, siblings, nephews, and nieces. But although I was grateful for their love and the generosity of a family I had longed for, I felt like a child among them. My overriding emotion was anxiety, the sort I had always endured when faced with an exam.

The following day I went to the civil registry office. I was searching for records relating to my parents' marriage; the official there dug out a large book that documented every local birth. Together we found the page that recorded my arrival; it also revealed that Johann and Helena were married in 1938—several years after my sister Tanja and brother Ludvig were born. It was a clue to the puzzle of the DNA tests; these had shown that while Ludvig's son, Rafael, was definitely my nephew, I was with equal certainty not a blood relative of Tanja's son, Marko. Given the fact that both Tanja and Ludvig had been born before my parents' wedding, the most likely explanation was that Tanja had a different father. The Matko family seemed to have more than its fair share of secrets.

The last remaining mystery was the other Erika. She had still not responded to my letters: nor, according to Maria, was she willing to speak to me in person.

I thought long and hard about what I should do. I had her address and decided that I would go to her apartment. It turned out to be on the fourth floor of a run-down building in a poor area of Rogaška Slatina. I knew Erika would be at home; the Matkos had told me she was too ill to walk down the stairs and so stayed inside every day. I found her letter box and the bell with her name on it. I wanted to press it, to be invited upstairs, and to see this enigmatic woman with my own eyes. I wanted to hold her, to speak with her and demand answers. I wanted, above all, to find the peace of mind that would come with confronting my other self.

But I did none of these things. As I stood on the street outside the building I realized that my anger was not merely unproductive but corrosive. I asked myself what right I had to force my needs on a sick and vulnerable woman who—just as much as me—had been a victim of the Nazis and of Lebensborn. I knew I had no such right, and that I had to learn not just to understand but to forgive. I walked quietly away.

TWO DAYS LATER, after a last meeting with my Slovenian family, I went home to Osnabrück. As I settled back into my life there I reflected on what the previous fifteen years had taught me. I seemed to have traveled a great distance, yet in truth my journey had really been a giant circle and I had arrived back at the very place where I began.

It had not been easy or painless, but I was glad—I *am* glad—to know the truth about Lebensborn and how I came to be caught up in it. I draw comfort from the extended "family" of those who were born or kidnapped into Himmler's experiment, and in the years since that first meeting in Hadamar, hundreds of us have discovered what we were searching for: the knowledge of who we are.

I am certain that I was once a Yugoslavian child called Erika Matko. I am certain that I was stolen from my family and I am grateful to have had the chance to be reunited with them. I wish, of course, that I could have met my biological mother; I wish I could remember her love for me and I am terribly saddened that I never had the chance to ask her about her life or the reason why she didn't search for me after the war.

BUT I DO not feel close to the Matkos in the way that families should feel close. Too much has happened; too great a separation of time and of place. There is a gulf between us that is more than simply one of language. I realize that I can no more understand what it means to have grown up in Yugoslavia than I can understand Slovenian.

In fact I feel much greater kinship with my late stepbrother, Hubertus. Rationally, I know that we were not blood relations, but in that realization lies the ultimate defeat of the Nazis' ideology. Blood is not important.

I can smile at that now. How did it take me so long to see something so obvious? I had spent a lifetime working with children burdened with physical or mental handicaps; I had seen how love and patience could overcome these disabilities. Nurture can always find a way to beat nature; the hammer does not necessarily shape the hand.

Ruefully, I reflected on the years I had allowed my life to be overshadowed. There is for all of us, I believe, a gap between what we want and what we can have, and regret flourishes in that gap. I had spent too long trapped in that disappointing no-man's-land between dreams and reality. I had lost sight of the fundamental truth that we are not defined by the facts of our birth, but instead by the choices we make throughout our life.

Mahatma Gandhi once said, *"The best way to find yourself is to lose yourself in the service of others."* It has taken me all my life to understand this. Yet although I am back exactly where I started, if I had not embarked on my journey, I don't think I would ever have worked this out. I now know who I was and who I am. Erika Matko was a Lebensborn baby, stolen from Yugoslavia, who disappeared in the madness of the Lebensborn program. Ingrid von Oelhafen is a German woman, a physical therapist who has brought help and comfort to generations of children.

My name is Ingrid von Oelhafen. It is also Erika Matko. Ingrid is German; Erika is from Yugoslavia. Both of them were me. But now? Now I am Ingrid Matko-von-Oelhafen. As I always have been.

# AFTERWORD

*That men do not learn very much from the lessons of
history is the most important of all the lessons of history.*

ALDOUS HUXLEY

THIS IS A story of what happened more than seventy years ago. It
would be easy to think of it only as history—easy, but wrong.

Since 1945 the world has not known a global conflict. Nor has
there been a criminal enterprise on the scale of the Third Reich, or
an ideology that so openly worships the mystic importance of pure
blood. But the key words are *global* and *openly*. The twisted creed that
holds that one person is inherently superior to another by virtue of his
race has not disappeared. Nor have the wars fought because of it.

From Southeast Asia to the Middle East, from Africa to the Bal-
kans, there have been those convinced that neighboring peoples,
races, or nations are inherently inferior. These post-Nazi *Untermen-
schen* are "other" and less deserving of respect, food, land, or life.

In the two generations since the Lebensborn experiment died in
the rubble of a devastated Europe, the world has known a succession
of smaller, more localized conflicts. Most have had, at their root, a
version of Himmler's belief in greater and lesser races.

This book is a personal memoir as well as an examination of history. It is being written at a time when the world is fracturing into ever greater hostility between nations, regions, or religions. Some of this hostility blossoms into nasty little wars—one ethnic group hacking another to pieces, one branch of a belief system blowing up those it deems to be lesser in the eyes of its God.

Particularly in Europe and on its borders, in countries that were once behind the Iron Curtain, politicians toy with nationalism, stoking the fires of hatred based on racial or historical inferiority. Not since 1945 has the continent—and beyond it, the world—been so dangerously divided.

The lesson of history is that no one learns the lesson of history. It is time we began.

# ACKNOWLEDGMENTS

FINDING MY ROOTS has been a long and rocky road. But I have met many wonderful people who accompanied me along the way.

I particularly want to say thank you to my best and most long-standing friend, Dorothee Schlüter. She has been with me from the first timid steps I took in my search for my origins. She has supported me mentally and emotionally and has been deeply involved as I progressed. Thanks are also due to Jutta Schröder, who has always been there with help and care.

I must express my gratitude to Dr. Georg Lilienthal for guiding me on my search, and to Josef Focks, who pushed me over and over again (as I hesitated) until at last I agreed to go to Slovenia.

To my friends in Lebensspuren, where I first met other children of the Lebensborn program: you, above all, know how important you have been.

For their company and support on my trips to Rogaška Slatina, I thank my friends Ute Grünwald, Ingrid Rätzmann, and Helga Lucas. And I am grateful to my Slovenian family for being so friendly and open.

I owe a special debt to Dr. Dorothee Schmitz-Köster. From the moment I met her she has been a great help. She not only encouraged my belief that this book could be written but has contributed her extensive knowledge of Lebensborn to its writing. She was also very good and sensible company on my last trip to Slovenia.

When Tim suggested this book, I made myself examine all the stages of my life. So much had been unknown and troublesome, but as we worked together I found the darkness that had enveloped me gradually disappearing. I also discovered that in the process of writing, I was able to "talk" to Helena, Johann, and even Erika Matko. I was able on the page (if not in reality) to ask "why?" I did not necessarily find all the answers. But these conversations—some of them heated!—helped me to forgive and to love life as it is.

Ingrid Matko-von-Oelhafen
Osnabrück, April 2015

THIS BOOK GREW out of a film I made in 2013.

I had heard of Lebensborn several years earlier and had tried—unsuccessfully—to persuade various television networks to commission a documentary about it. Finally, Channel 5 agreed to fund a sixty-minute film: I am indebted to its commissioning editor, Simon Raikes, for seeing the importance of the story and backing it.

I met Ingrid while researching the program; she agreed to be filmed and was immensely generous when I was unable, for reasons of space, to include her story within the documentary. She was also kind enough to listen when I subsequently suggested that we should write a book about her extraordinary and brave journey to discover the truth about Lebensborn and her past.

Neither that film nor this book could have emerged without the efforts and encouragement of Dr. Dorothee Schmitz-Köster. The Lebensborn children have no greater champion than Dorothee, and her commitment to telling their stories in her own books (sadly published only in Germany) has been crucial in bringing Himmler's shadowy organization into the light.

Many sources were helpful in cross-checking and verifying the Lebensborn survivors' stories, including: "Nazi 'Selective Breeding,'" *The Times* (14 December 1943); "Hitler's Children," Joshua Hammer, *Newsweek International* (20 March 2000); "Nazi Past Haunts 'Aryan' Children," Kate Bissell, BBC News website (13 June 2005); "Sixty of Hitler's children meet," Associated Press (5 November 2006); "Eight people, products of the Lebensborn programme to propagate Aryan traits, met to exchange their stories," Mark Landler, *New York Times* (7 November 2006); "Nazi program to breed master Race," David Crossland, *Der Spiegel* (8 March 2007); "Documents detail Nazis' drive for racial purity," Melissa Eddy, Associated Press (6 April 2007); "Man kidnapped by SS discovers true identity," *Daily Telegraph* (6 January 2009); "Stolen by the Nazis: The tragic tale of 12,000 blue-eyed blond children taken by the SS to create an Aryan super-race," *Daily Mail* (9 January 2009); "Stolen Children," Gitta Sereny, *Talk* Magazine (2009); "Third Reich poster child," Titus Chalk, *ExBerliner* (22 November 2010); Tone Ferenc: Documents relating to the Nazi occupation of Yugoslavia at http://karawan kengrenze.at/ferenc/index.php?r=documentshow&id=249.

Our thanks are also due to our British publishers, Elliott and Thompson, for so enthusiastically supporting this book, and to our editor there, Olivia Bays; her cool-headed advice significantly improved our manuscript.

Similarly, Andrew Lownie is the very model of a perfect literary agent. His initial guidance, and thereafter his relationship with publishers across the world, has ensured that this story will be read in countries as far apart as Finland, Italy, Poland, Romania, Turkey, and the United States.

Finally, I could not write without the love and support of my partner, Mia Pennal. After a lifetime of searching I was lucky enough to be found. *Cursum Perficio*: my journey ends here.

Tim Tate
Wiltshire, April 2015

# BIBLIOGRAPHY

Bessel, Richard, *Germany 1945: From War to Peace* (London: Simon & Schuster, 2009).

Clay, Catrine and Michael Leapman, *Master Race: The Lebensborn Experiment in Nazi Germany* (London: Coronet, 1995).

Hillel, Marc and Clarissa Henry, *Of Pure Blood* (New York: McGraw-Hill, 1976).

Owen, James, *Nuremberg: Evil on Trial* (London: Headline, 2006).

Schmitz-Köster, Dorothee, *Lebenslang Lebensborn* (Munich: Piper Verlag, 2012).

Taylor, Frederick, *Exorcising Hitler: The Occupation and Denazification of Germany* (New York: Bloomsbury, 2011).

Weale, Adrian, *The SS: A New History* (London: Little, Brown, 2010).